Lucent Books, P.O. Box 289011, San Diego, CA 92198-9011

Titles in The American War Library series include:

World War II
Hitler and the Nazis
Kamikazes
Leaders and Generals
Life as a POW
Life of an American Soldier in
 Europe
Strategic Battles in Europe
Strategic Battles in the Pacific
The War at Home
Weapons of War

The Civil War
Leaders of the North and South
Life Among the Soldiers and
 Cavalry
Lincoln and the Abolition of
 Slavery
Strategic Battles
Weapons of War

Library of Congress Cataloging-in-Publication Data

Rice, Earle, Jr.
    Strategic battles in the Pacific / Earle Rice, Jr.
        p.   cm.—(The American war library series)
    Includes bibliographical references and index.
    Summary: Discusses strategic battles in the Pacific during
World War II, including Bataan and Corregidor, Guadalcanal,
Tarawa, Leyte Gulf, Iwo Jima, and Okinawa.
    ISBN 1-56006-537-0 (lib. : alk. paper)
    1. World War, 1939–1945—Campaigns—Pacific Area—
Juvenile literature. [1. World War, 1939–1945—Campaigns—
Pacific Area.] I. Title. II. Series.
D767.9.R53 2000
940.54'26—dc21   99-045479

⋆ **Contents** ⋆

A Nation Forged by War

The United States, like many nations, was forged and defined by war. Despite Benjamin Franklin's opinion that "There never was a good war or a bad peace," the United States owes its very existence to the War of Independence, one to which Franklin wholeheartedly subscribed. The country forged by war in 1776 was tempered and made stronger by the Civil War in the 1860s.

The Texas Revolution, the Mexican-American War, and the Spanish-American War expanded the country's borders and gave it overseas possessions. These wars made the United States a world power, but this status came with a price, as the nation became a key but reluctant player in both World War I and World War II.

Each successive war further defined the country's role on the world stage. Following World War II, U.S. foreign policy redefined itself to focus on the role of defender, not only of the freedom of its own citizens, but also of the freedom of people everywhere. During the cold war that followed World War II until the collapse of the Soviet Union, defending the world meant fighting communism. This goal, manifested in the Korean and Vietnam conflicts, proved elusive, and soured the American public on its achievability. As the United States emerged as the world's sole superpower, American foreign policy has been guided less by national interest and more on protecting international human rights. But as involvement in Somalia and Kosovo prove, this goal has been equally elusive.

As a result, the country's view of itself changed. Bolstered by victories in World Wars I and II, Americans first relished the role of protector. But, as war followed war in a seemingly endless procession, Americans began to doubt their leaders, their motives, and themselves. The Vietnam War especially caused people to question the validity of sending its young people to die in places where they were not particularly wanted and for people who did not seem especially grateful.

While the most obvious changes brought about by America's wars have been geopolitical in nature, many other aspects of society have been touched. War often does not bring about change directly, but acts instead like the catalyst in a chemical reaction, accelerating changes already in progress.

Some of these changes have been societal. The role of women in the United States had been slowly changing, but World War II put thousands into the workforce and into uniform. They might have gone back to being housewives after the war, but equality, once experienced, would not be forgotten.

Likewise, wars have accelerated technological change. The necessity for faster airplanes and a more destructive bomb led to the development of jet planes and nuclear energy. Artificial fibers developed for parachutes in the 1940s were used in the clothing of the 1950s.

Lucent Books' American War Library covers key wars in the development of the nation. Each war is covered in several volumes, to allow for more detail, context, and to provide volumes on often neglected subjects, such as the kamikazes of World War II, or weapons used in the Civil War. As with all Lucent Books, notes, annotated bibliographies, and appendixes such as glossaries give students a launching point for further research. In addition, sidebars and archival photographs enhance the text. Together, each volume in The American War Library will aid students in understanding how America's wars have shaped and changed its politics, economics, and society.

Selection of Battles

Japan's surprise attack on U.S. military installations at Pearl Harbor and elsewhere on 7 December 1941 spearheaded a series of Japanese aggressions across the Pacific and in the Far East. In the flash of a Sunday morning bomb burst, the United States found itself thrust into the most destructive and wide-ranging conflict in history. The next day, U.S. president Franklin D. Roosevelt called on Congress to declare war on Japan. Congress complied. And Americans everywhere took up arms to fight for their very survival. They fought in every clime and wartime arena around the globe, in the greatest war humankind ever inflicted upon itself. This, then, is the story of the war in the Pacific Theater—on the land, at sea, and in the air.

Six classic battles have been carefully selected for portrayal in the pages ahead. Each battle has been chosen for its strategic importance and relevance to the unfolding American battle plan and for how it interacts with the other five battles. Collectively, these battles are intended to chart the course of the war and to monitor the extraordinary wartime achievements of each U.S. military service.

The destroyer USS Shaw *explodes after being struck by a Japanese bomb during the attack on Pearl Harbor.*

Military Twenty-Four-Hour Clock

Military times are used throughout the book. This key, showing familiar A.M. and P.M. times paired with the corresponding time on the twenty-four-hour clock, may be helpful in learning the system.

A.M.	24	P.M.	24
1	0100	1	1300
2	0200	2	1400
3	0300	3	1500
4	0400	4	1600
5	0500	5	1700
6	0600	6	1800
7	0700	7	1900
8	0800	8	2000
9	0900	9	2100
10	1000	10	2200
11	1100	11	2300
12	1200	12	2400

The battle for Bataan-Corregidor (2 January–6 May 1942) resulted in a resounding Japanese victory and the greatest capitulation in the history of the U.S. Army. After nearly six months of constant fighting (commencing with the Japanese invasion of Luzon on 10 December 1941), U.S. major general Jonathan Wainwright, General Douglas MacArthur's successor in the Philippines, surrendered to the Japanese. In a final message to President Roosevelt, Wainwright wrote: "With broken heart and head bowed in sadness but not in shame I report to your Excellency that today I must arrange terms for the surrender of the fortified islands of Manila Bay."[1] Humiliated by the demoralizing American defeat, General MacArthur vowed to return to the Philippines, and he based much of his strategy for the rest of the Pacific War on keeping his promise.

Guadalcanal, in the Solomon Islands, claims a unique place in history as the site of the first U.S. offensive land action against the Japanese (7 August 1942–7 February 1943). This hard-won American victory provided a huge lift to sagging American spirits and greatly improved the Allies' strategic situation. It marked the first defeat of the Imperial Japanese Army on land in World War II. Also, notes combat correspondent Frank O. Hough, of the U.S. Marine Corps, "It demonstrated clearly to the world at large that the Japanese soldier was something less than the superman he had been pictured on the strength of his early, easy victories."[2]

Later in the year (20–23 November 1943), Americans took the war to the Japanese at Tarawa, in the Gilbert Islands, securing the heavily defended island fortress in seventy-six hours of savage fighting. Three thousand marine casualties paid the high cost of coral, prompting war correspondent Robert Sherrod to write, "It was inconceivable to most Marines that . . . they could be responsible for dimming the bright reputation of their corps. The Marines simply assumed that they were the world's best fighting men."[3] The capture of Tarawa provided a strategic air base for the next phase of Allied operations and opened the door for the American drive across the Central Pacific.

Eleven months later (23–26 October 1944), the U.S. Navy, in support of General MacArthur's pledged return to the Philippines, virtually destroyed the Imperial Japanese Navy in a naval battle at Leyte Gulf. The actions of the U.S. 3rd and 7th Fleets, in Admiral William F. Halsey's words, "resulted in [the] utter failure of the Japanese plan to prevent the re-occupation of the Philippines" and in "the crushing defeat of the Japanese Fleet."[4] This decisive sea battle, cited by many as the greatest naval engagement ever fought, cleared the way for U.S. forces to extend their Philippine conquests northward and drive relentlessly closer to Japan itself.

The incredibly fortified volcanic island of Iwo Jima, 760 miles south of Tokyo, stood next in the path of the advancing Allies. Fleet Admiral Chester W. Nimitz wanted to seize the island's air bases for use in a stepped-up air campaign against Japan proper. In one of the hardest fought battles of the Pacific War, American marines, at the cost of some twenty-six thousand casualties, captured the island bastion in just over a month (19 February–26 March 1945). Marine lieutenant general Holland M. Smith later commented on the military lesson learned there. "Iwo Jima," he said, "proved the falsity of the theory that regiments or battalions that are decimated can never win battles."[5]

Six days later, U.S. soldiers and marines, backed by a huge U.S. naval armada, landed on Okinawa to begin the battle for the last essential stepping-stone to the Japanese homeland (1 April–22 June 1945). Lieutenant General Mitsuru Ushijima, commander of the Japanese 32nd Army defense force on the island, ordered his troops to fight to the death and promised that "our weapons exhausted, our blood will bathe the earth."[6] Despite the tenacious defense of the Japanese defenders and several weeks of terrorizing kamikaze attacks on the U.S. fleet, the Americans prevailed. The southernmost Japanese home island of Kyushu now lay only 350 miles to the north.

Bone-tired veterans of the Okinawa campaign now girded themselves for the anticipated invasion of the Japanese home islands. But they had already fought the last battle of the Pacific War.

★ Chapter 1 ★

World War II in the Pacific

"Should hostilities break out between Japan and the United States, it would not be enough that we take Guam and the Philippines, nor even Hawaii and San Francisco. To make victory certain, we would have to march into Washington and dictate the terms of peace in the White House."
—Admiral Isoroku Yamamoto, commander in chief of Japan's Combined Fleet (quoted in Gordon W. Prange, *At Dawn We Slept*)

At 0753, from high above Barber's Point on the Hawaiian island of Oahu, Commander Mitsuo Fuchida's voice rang out elatedly in a radioed message to his superiors: *"Tora! Tora! Tora!"* ("Tiger! Tiger! Tiger!").[7] This coded redundancy signaled to the entire Imperial Japanese Navy that his attack wave had caught the U.S. Pacific Fleet unawares. Two minutes later, the first Japanese bomb dropped on Pearl Harbor. It was Sunday morning, December 7, 1941.

Over the next two hours, two waves of Japanese planes sank 6 battleships and damaged 2 others and sank or damaged 12 other ships. They further destroyed 164

U.S. aircraft and damaged another 128. Altogether 2,403 American soldiers, sailors, marines, airmen, and civilians were killed. The Japanese sustained relatively light losses: 29 aircraft and 6 submarines, 5 of them midgets. When the attackers returned to their aircraft carriers, the once-proud U.S. Pacific Fleet lay blanketed under billowing towers of oil-blackened smoke.

What had appeared at first to be an awesome strategic victory for Japan came to be seen over time for what it was: a short-term tactical victory. The Pacific Fleet rose up to fight another day. In the long term, the attack succeeded in galvanizing the will and fighting spirit of the American people and unleashing the military and industrial might of the United States, thus assuring Japan's defeat.

But for the first six months of the war, America and its allies were destined to suffer the pain and humiliation of multiple defeats in the Pacific and Southeast Asia.

The First Six Months

The attack on Pearl Harbor triggered a chain reaction of Japanese aggressions across the Pacific and Southeast Asia. Japanese forces struck the Philippines, Malaya, Borneo, Thailand, Guam, Wake Atoll, and the Gilbert Islands. Japanese planes attacked Hong Kong, Shanghai, Manila, and Singapore. And on it went. Japan expanded its empire like a giant octopus spreading its tentacles.

Wake Island (Atoll) fell on 23 December; Hong Kong, two days later. On Christmas Day, the Hong Kong newspaper *South China Morning Post* carried a holiday message from Sir Mark Young, the island's governor:

> In pride and admiration I send my greetings this Christmas Day to all those who are working so nobly and so well to sustain Hong Kong against the assault of the enemy. Fight on. Hold fast for King and Empire. God bless you all in this your finest hour.[8]

The sunken battleship USS Arizona *burns after the attack. 1,177 sailors and marines died aboard this ship, which is now a memorial.*

The defenders of the island crown colony laid down their arms and surrendered to the invaders at 1515 that afternoon.

Singapore, the so-called impregnable British fortress and naval base, surrendered to the Japanese on 15 February 1942. British prime minister Winston Churchill called the collapse of the island stronghold "the worst disaster and capitulation in British history."[9]

Java, in the Dutch East Indies, surrendered on 9 March. In a last broadcast, a commercial radio station in Java reported, "We are shutting down now. Goodbye till better times. Long live the Queen!"[10] Four days after the fall of Java, Japanese forces landed in the Solomon Islands.

A Great Help

When Commander Mitsuo Fuchida, leader of the first attack wave at Pearl Harbor, returned to the carrier *Akagi*, he urged a second attack against Pearl's dockyards and fuel tanks. The carriers *Soryu* and *Hiryu* had already signaled their readiness to launch another attack. But Vice Admiral Chuichi Nagumo, commander of the Japanese aircraft carrier striking force, was concerned that the U.S. carriers not found at berth in Pearl Harbor might be looking for his own carriers at that very moment.

Rather than jeopardize his fleet with an unscheduled second attack, Nagumo heeded the advice of his chief of staff, Rear Admiral Ryunosuke Kusaka. "We should retire as planned," Kusaka said, as noted by John Toland in *The Rising Sun*. Nagumo nodded affirmatively, and the carrier task force set course for a leisurely return to Japan.

In fairness to Admiral Nagumo, he had fulfilled his mission, to knock the Pacific Fleet out of action for about six months. This would enable Japan to carry out its projected conquest of the Western Pacific, unhindered by the U.S. Navy on its flank. Nevertheless, several American admirals, including Fleet Admiral Chester W. Nimitz, thought Nagumo's decision not to risk a second attack was a critical mistake.

According to Gordon W. Prange in *At Dawn We Slept*, Nimitz later remarked, "The fact that the Japanese did not return to Pearl Harbor and complete the job was the greatest help to us, for they left their principal enemy with the time to catch his breath, restore his morale, and rebuild his forces."

Vice Admiral Chuichi Nagumo's decision not to attack Pearl Harbor's dockyards and fuel tanks gave the Americans time to rebuild.

General MacArthur had directed the U.S. defense of the Philippines until President Roosevelt ordered him to leave for Australia on the night of 11–12 March. Upon his arrival in Darwin, MacArthur issued his famous statement, "I came through and I shall return."[11] He then assumed the duties of supreme commander Allied forces, Pacific.

Bataan fell on 9 April; Corregidor on 6 May. Although the defense of Bataan and Corregidor failed to delay the Japanese timetable of conquest, as originally thought, it had a significant effect on how the United States conducted the Pacific War from that point on.

The Americans now divided the Pacific into two theaters of operation. General

MacArthur took command of the Southwest Pacific Area, consisting of Australia, New Guinea, the Philippines, Borneo, the Bismarck archipelago, and much of the Dutch East Indies. (He wanted command of the entire Pacific Theater, but the navy resisted too strongly and a compromise was reached.) Japan, of course, controlled most of these territories.

Admiral Nimitz, in addition to his Pacific Fleet command, assumed responsibility for all forces and operations in the rest of the Pacific. With these commands in place, the Americans began to fight back.

Turning Points

In six months of lightning thrusts in the Western Pacific and Southeast Asia, the Japanese had vastly extended their area of domination. It extended from the Kuril Islands in the north, southeast to the Gilbert Islands, and westward to India in a sweeping arc through the Solomons, New Guinea, and the Dutch East Indies. They called this vast region under Japanese control the Greater East Asia Co-Prosperity Sphere, an area devoid of all Western influence. At the start of the second six months of the war, however, impending Allied offensives were about to turn the sphere's boundaries into a Japanese defense perimeter.

In the Battle of Midway (4–7 June 1942), a U.S. carrier task force turned back the Japanese fleet and tipped the balance of sea power in favor of the Americans. They never relinquished it. Most naval strategists and historians recognize the Battle of Midway as the turning point in the Pacific naval war. Back in his Hawaiian headquarters, Admiral Nimitz reported the Japanese defeat in a battle communique. He could not resist ending it on a humorous note: "Perhaps we will be forgiven if we claim we are about midway to our objective."[12]

After Midway, the initiative shifted to the Americans. The U.S Joint Chiefs of Staff now devised a master battle plan that provided for a two-pronged offensive directed at the heart of Japan. In keeping with the co-commander system in the Pacific, General MacArthur's command was directed to battle its way up the northern coast of New Guinea and then on to the Philippines. Meanwhile, Admiral Nimitz's command was to strike across the seemingly endless island groups and atolls in the Central Pacific.

On 7 August, two months to the day after the end of the battle at Midway, the reinforced 1st Marine Division landed on Guadalcanal in the Solomons. Their mission was to seize a Japanese airfield under construction and secure the island for Allied use in future offensive operations. The marines met only moderate enemy resistance at first and secured the airfield readily. But the Japanese poured reinforcements into the island, and a series of fierce battles followed in the jungles and offshore.

Japanese soldiers and sailors believed that their only options in combat were victory or *gyokusai*—glorious self-annihilation. When victory ceased to be an option, their

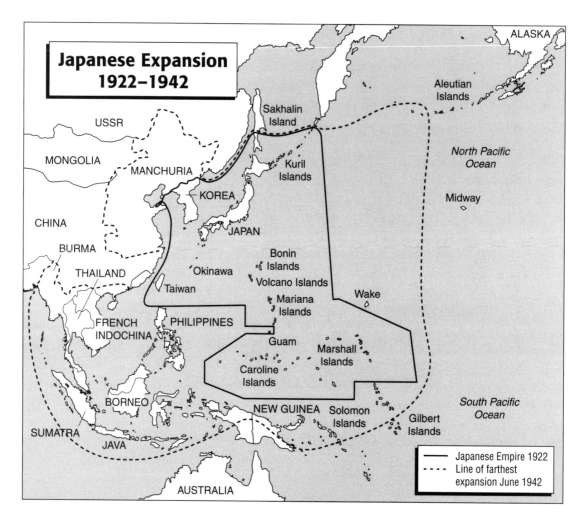

Japanese Expansion 1922–1942

ALASKA

USSR

MONGOLIA

MANCHURIA

KOREA

CHINA

JAPAN

BURMA

THAILAND

Okinawa

Taiwan

FRENCH INDOCHINA

PHILIPPINES

BORNEO

SUMATRA

JAVA

AUSTRALIA

Sakhalin Island

Kuril Islands

Bonin Islands

Volcano Islands

Mariana Islands

Guam

Caroline Islands

NEW GUINEA

Solomon Islands

Marshall Islands

Gilbert Islands

Wake

Aleutian Islands

North Pacific Ocean

Midway

South Pacific Ocean

——— Japanese Empire 1922
- - - Line of farthest expansion June 1942

belief in *gyokusai* required them to fight to the death. They gained a false sense of immortality in their further belief that they would live on through the spirit of the emperor or *kokutai*—the national body. "It is ironic that the more desperate the situation Japanese soldiers were in," writes Japanese historian Yuki Tanaka, "the more fiercely they would fight and show loyalty toward the emperor so that

their spirit might live on." [13] This was the enemy.

The U.S. Army 25th Infantry Division relieved the exhausted and decimated marines in December, and the fighting continued until it ended in an American victory on 7 February 1943. Marine commander Major General Alexander Vandegrift later summed up the campaign this way:

We were as well trained and as well armed as our peacetime experience allowed us to be. We needed combat to tell us how effective our training, our doctrines, and our weapons had been. We tested them against the enemy, and we found that they worked.[14]

Military analysts now view the battle for Guadalcanal—a joint U.S. Army–Navy–Marine Corps operation—as a major turning point in the Pacific War from which Japan never recovered.

The Island-Hopping Campaigns: Phase I

After Guadalcanal, the Americans and their allies abandoned their defensive posture and set about the formidable task of reclaiming all of the territories lost to the Japanese thus far. By then, the Japanese were solidly entrenched in many of their island holdings. The task of uprooting and ousting them would not be an easy one.

Experience gained in the Guadalcanal campaign in air and naval bombardment, amphibious landings, and jungle fighting would prove invaluable to the Allied forces in the months ahead. Also, a new strategy of bypassing and isolating heavily defended enemy positions to reach and attack weaker installations worked extremely well. The Allies now embarked on the first phase of two island-hopping campaigns aimed straight at the heart of Tokyo.

During the next eight months of 1943, Allied forces, primarily Americans under Vice Admiral William F. Halsey, swept through the Solomons and nearby island groups in the Southwest Pacific Area. Halsey bypassed enemy strongholds such as Kolombangara, allowing them to wither on the vine with their supply lines cut, and concentrated on securing weaker objectives. Air and naval bombardments were now used in more generous measures before the experienced jungle fighters stormed ashore. Meanwhile, MacArthur's U.S.-Australian troops were slogging forward up the New Guinea coastline.

In the Central Pacific, U.S. Marines struck at Tarawa, in the Gilbert Islands. The marines secured the atoll after seventy-six hours of savage fighting, but at a cost of more than three thousand dead and

U.S. marines display a Japanese flag captured on Guadalcanal. Japan never fully recovered from its defeat in this campaign.

wounded. On 22 November, marine Major General Julian C. Smith reported:

> Progress slow and extremely costly. Complete occupation will take at least five days more. Naval and air bombardment a great help but does not take out emplacements.[15]

The general had underestimated his marines. Betio fell the next day. The marines' high casualty rate seriously shocked the American public, but Nimitz's first island stepping-stone had fallen, along with Makin Island, to the north of Tarawa. Control of the Gilberts provided the Americans with an advanced air base in the Central Pacific and cleared the way for the next phase of operations.

In December 1943, U.S. soldiers and marines struck at Arawe and Cape Gloucester in New Britain and captured Long Island to the west. The year—and Phase 1 of the island-hopping campaigns—ended with Allied forces in the Pacific advancing steadily.

The Island-Hopping Campaigns: Phase 2

Both branches of the island-hopping campaigns gained great momentum in 1944. General MacArthur's U.S.-Australian troops continued to press forward along New Guinea's fifteen-hundred-mile northern coast, while Admiral Nimitz's amphibious corps (the ships and men of the landing force) were capturing the Marshall Islands.

Back in New Guinea, three U.S. infantry divisions landed at Hollandia on 22 April and began the final battle for MacArthur's first step toward the Philippines. The Americans came away victors on 27 August, after virtually destroying the Japanese 18th Army.

On 15 June, while U.S. B-29 Superfortresses were bombing Tokyo and American submarines were wreaking havoc on Japanese shipping up and down the Western Pacific, U.S. Marines began landing on Saipan, in the Marianas—the inner ring of Japanese defenses. To help repulse the Americans, the Japanese rushed in a large carrier attack force. A U.S. carrier force met it head-on in the Battle of the Philippine Sea and scored another decisive victory.

During the air fighting, one U.S. pilot quipped, "Hell, this is like an old-time turkey shoot!"[16] Veteran navy men still refer to the air battle as the Great Marianas Turkey Shoot. Saipan fell on 9 July.

By mid-August, Nimitz's forces had all but cleared the Marianas—Saipan, Tinian, and Guam—and Tinian soon served as an air base for B-29 bombers bound for Japan. By then, the forces of MacArthur and Halsey had gained almost total control over New Guinea and the Solomons.

On 15 September, American marines and soldiers struck simultaneously at Peleliu and Angaur in the Palaus and at Morotai in the northern Moluccas, respectively. The capture of Morotai set the stage for MacArthur's next strike at the Philippine island of Leyte.

U.S. Navy pilots aboard the carrrier USS Lexington celebrate their victories during the Great Marianas Turkey Shoot in June 1944 (above). General Douglas MacArthur returns to the Philippines on 20 October 1944.

On 20 October, the general kept his promise. He waded ashore from a small boat and announced over a microphone in a drizzling rain, "People of the Philippines, I have returned."[17] The battle for the island officially ended on 25 December.

At the start of the Battle of Leyte, a complicated Japanese attempt to smash the U.S. invasion fleet erupted into the largest naval engagement in history—the Battle of Leyte Gulf (23–26 October). In several separate sea battles, made all the more notable by the introduction of Japan's suicide kamikaze corps, U.S. naval forces destroyed most of what remained of the Imperial Japanese Navy.

The Island-Hopping Campaigns: Final Phase

Early in 1945, the Allies, like a boxer sensing a knockout of his opponent, rushed in for the kill. Elements of the U.S. 6th Army landed at Lingayen Gulf in Luzon on 7 January and commenced the Battle of Luzon (9 January–1 July), the largest ground campaign of the Pacific War. In mid-March, the Americans pressed northward into northern Luzon, where determined Japanese resistance continued until the end of the war.

Meanwhile, the 3rd, 4th, and 5th Marine Divisions seized Iwo Jima—one of the Volcano Islands, 760 miles southeast of Tokyo—for use as a B-29 air base in the strategic bombing campaign against Japan. In just under a month of some of the fiercest fighting of the war (19 February–26 March), the marines controlled the volcanic isle.

Reflecting later on the entrenched defenders, Admiral Raymond A. Spruance commented, "In view of the character of the defenses and the stubborn resistance encountered, it is fortunate that less seasoned or less resolute troops were not committed."[18] The fall of Iwo Jima moved the B-29s to Tokyo's doorstep and prevented Japanese aircraft from using its air bases in operations against the Allied invasion fleet at Okinawa.

Now, only Okinawa—one of the Ryukyu Islands, 350 miles south of mainland Japan—stood between the advancing Allies on the ocean road to the Japanese home islands. American soldiers and marines, supported by a massive Allied invasion fleet, landed at Okinawa on Easter Sunday, 1 April 1945, to begin the last great battle of World War II. After two and a half months of bitter, bitter fighting, at a huge cost to both sides, Okinawa finally fell on 22 June.

Due to the suicidal attacks of Japanese kamikazes, the Okinawa campaign was the only amphibious operation of the war in which more seamen were killed than either soldiers or marines. After taking repeated kamikaze hits, Admiral Marc Mitscher was heard to say, "Any more of this and there will be hair growing on this old bald

The carrier USS Bunker Hill *burns after a kamikaze strike at Okinawa. As a result of attacks like this, more American sailors died at Okinawa than either soldiers or marines.*

head."[19] The fanatical Japanese resistance played a major role in President Harry S Truman's decision to use atomic weapons.

On 6 August 1945, a U.S. B-29 dropped an atomic bomb on the Japanese city of Hiroshima. Three days later, a second atomic bomb sealed Japan's fate at Nagasaki. Japan surrendered on 14 August and signed the official surrender documents aboard the U.S. battleship *Missouri*, in Tokyo Bay, on 2 September 1945. And the greatest war in history ended.

Bataan and Corregidor: A Gallant Defense

"Seldom if ever in all military history had men fought more magnificently than had our own soldiers, sailors, marines and Philippine Scouts in this desperate struggle which every one of them knew was, in the end, hopeless."
—Lieutenant Colonel Warren J. Clear, USA
(in "The Gallant Defense of the Philippines,"
Reader's Digest Illustrated Story of World War II)

It should not have happened, but it did. On 8 December 1941 (7 December in Hawaii) at 1215, a Japanese air armada of 108 twin-engined bombers and 34 fighter planes from airfields in Formosa (Taiwan) darkened the skies over the Clark Field–Iba air base complex near Manila, the capital of the Philippines. Moments later, a torrent of bombs rained down on the U.S. airstrips, shattering hangars and barracks and pulverizing runways and standing aircraft from one end of the complex to the other. Then the fighters soared in at near-ground level and strafed everything and everyone in sight, slaughtering pilots, aircrews, and other base personnel indis-criminately. The raiders destroyed 18 of 35 B-17s ("Flying Fortresses") and 56 fighters, plus a number of other aircraft. Only one U.S. fighter squadron made it off the ground to challenge the Japanese intruders. The American pilots knocked down 7 enemy fighters but were themselves almost obliterated. When the bombers left, Clark-Iba lay in a flaming shambles, with twisted wreckage and maimed bodies strewn about everywhere. In one fateful hour, the Japanese had wiped out half of the U.S. air forces in the Philippines. Lieutenant Colonel Warren J. Clear, USA, a member of General Douglas MacArthur's staff who survived the attack, later wrote, "That raid and the simultaneous attack on other airfields

As explosions erupt below, a Japanese twin-engined bomber flies over a target in the Philippines on 8 December 1941. The attack on Clark Field–Iba air base complex wiped out most of MacArthur's air force.

near Manila sealed the fate of Luzon and Corregidor."[20]

Tragically, ample evidence suggests that the Americans should have been on the alert and expecting just such a raid. Instead, when the Japanese planes struck, they caught most of the U.S. planes on the ground being serviced while many of their pilots and aircrews were at lunch. The B-17s had returned to base for refueling after a fruitless morning patrol over northern Luzon. But the need to refuel, given the circumstances, hardly excuses base personnel's failure to remain alert for all possibilities. News of the sneak attack on Pearl

Harbor had reached Manila at 0230 that morning and was confirmed three hours later. Airfields in northern Luzon had been bombed at 0930. Moreover, Major General Lewis H. Brereton, commander of MacArthur's Far East Air Force, had received a telephone call from Army Air Force chief General Henry H. ("Hap") Arnold in Washington warning him of a likely Japanese attack. Despite all forewarnings, when the Japanese bombers arrived at Clark–Iba, they found practically all of the U.S. aircraft sitting like ducks in a row on their airstrips. Why the base failed to maintain a full-alert status and who bears responsibility for that breach of vigilance remain moot to this day. In any case, MacArthur, faced with the loss of most of his air force, radically revised his defense strategy for the Philippines.

Defensive and Offensive Strategies

In the fall of 1935, General Douglas Mac-Arthur, after having served as army chief of staff, arrived in the Philippines to serve as "military adviser" to Manuel Quezon, first president of the newly established Philippine commonwealth. The Philippines, ceded to the United States after the 1898 war with Spain, were at that time scheduled for full independence in ten years. Mac-Arthur, who had begun his military career there as a second lieutenant of engineers in 1903, felt an emotional attachment to the islands. Due to retire in nine years, he viewed his new duties of creating and training a Filipino defense force as a fitting way to crown his service career. He worked with a passion to build an elite army, openly boasting, "By 1946 I will make the islands a Pacific Switzerland [an impregnable domain] that would cost any invader 500,000 men, three years, and more than five billion dollars to conquer."[21]

His boast, in the opinion of most U.S. military minds, contained more style than substance. The Philippines, 7,100-odd islands comprising some 115,651 square miles, stretch 1,152 miles from north to south and 688 miles from east to west. They are inundated with inland seas and many bays and harbors formed by irregular coastlines and are forested with dense jungles. Only an extreme optimist would consider them defensible by the small forces available.

As great a general as MacArthur may have been—and his detractors abound—his judgment in this instance is open to serious question. Yet his great confidence in the army of his creation (and likely some egotism) blinded him to the reality of its

true capability. He apparently convinced himself that his "Swiss-style citizen's army"[22] could defend all seventy-one hundred islands of the Philippines. (The Swiss employed a compulsory militia utilizing all

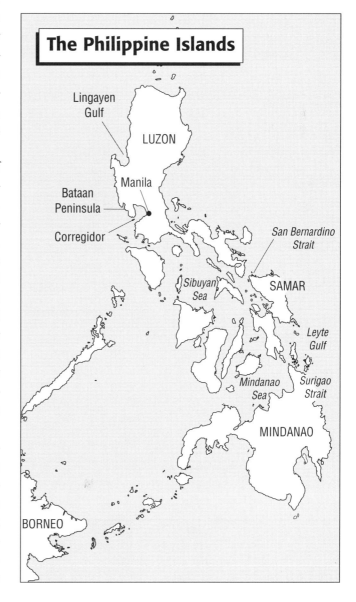

The Philippine Islands

Lingayen Gulf

LUZON

Manila

Bataan Peninsula

Corregidor

San Bernardino Strait

Sibuyan Sea

SAMAR

Leyte Gulf

Mindanao Sea

Surigao Strait

MINDANAO

BORNEO

able-bodied men between the ages of eight and sixty.)

Some of MacArthur's aides, including Major Dwight D. Eisenhower, doubted his judgment. And Admiral Thomas C. Hart, chief of the small U.S. Asiatic Fleet, confided to his spouse, "Douglas is not completely sane, and may not have been for some considerable time."[23] But evidence suggests a strong personality clash between the two men. MacArthur was a known egotist but certainly not a madman.

Throughout the 1920s and 1930s, American defense planners had held that such a defense strategy bordered on impossible. Accordingly, they developed a contingency plan over the years, identified as War Plan Orange-3 (WPO-3). This plan called for the Americans to concentrate their (and the Filipino) forces in the Bataan Peninsula and defend its narrow neck and the island fortresses of Corregidor and Fort Drum in the entrance to Manila Bay until the U.S. Pacific Fleet arrived with reinforcements. But on 26 July 1941, Washington, for whatever reason, scrapped WPO-3 in favor of MacArthur's plan to defend the entire archipelago.

Many military analysts now consider the move to have been not simply a show of confidence in MacArthur's strategical acumen but a warning to Japan—who had recently occupied southern Indochina (Vietnam)—that any further expansion southward would lead to war with the United States. To underscore its warning, Washington sent reinforcements to the Philippines and elevated MacArthur from his advisory rank of field marshal to commander of U.S. Army Forces Far East on 26 July.

By December 1941, MacArthur's Far East army numbered some 130,000 men—22,400 U.S. regulars (including 12,000 crack American-Filipino Philippine Scouts), 3,000 Philippine Constabulary (national police), and the 107,000-man Philippine Army, still only partially organized, trained, and equipped.

For air support, MacArthur relied on General Brereton's Philippine-based Far East Air Force of 277 aircraft, including 36 B-17 Flying Fortresses and 100 P-40 Warhawks, the most powerful concentration of U.S. airpower outside Hawaii. Ad-

A B-17 Flying Fortress patrols the skies over islands near Luzon. Thirty-six Fortresses were based in the Philippines at the start of the war.

miral Hart's Asiatic Fleet, consisting of 1 heavy cruiser, 2 light cruisers, 13 destroyers, 28 submarines, and several squadrons of patrol-torpedo (PT) boats, represented the only naval support immediately available to MacArthur.

MacArthur organized his forces into four commands that together covered the entire archipelago. He assigned the critical area of northern Luzon to Major General Jonathan M. Wainwright, allocating four divisions to him—about half of his available manpower—to repel an anticipated invasion at Lingayen Gulf. Brigadier General George M. Parker's smaller South Luzon Force took up positions south of Manila, with other elements of MacArthur's remaining forces deployed on the islands of Cebu, the Visayas, and Mindanao. But both MacArthur and Wainwright expected the decisive battle to be fought at Lingayen Gulf.

MacArthur intended to meet an invasion at Lingayen with a strong counterattack at the beaches, while neutralizing enemy air support with a B-17 air strike against Japanese air bases in Formosa. The air attack never materialized, however, because of a delay in the chain of command. The three principals most responsible for carrying out the B-17 strike—MacArthur, his chief of staff, Major General Richard K. Sutherland, and Brereton—each blamed one or both of the others for not proceeding with the mission.

MacArthur, in his postwar writings, disclaimed all responsibility for the performance (or lack thereof) of his air force. "Our air forces in the Philippines, containing many antiquated models, were hardly more than a token force," he noted. "They were hopelessly outnumbered and never had a chance of winning." Yet, in November 1941, he had eagerly sought the task of "conducting strong offensive air operations."[24]

As a last-ditch defense contingency, MacArthur planned to reactivate the WPO-3 plan and withdraw his forces into the mountainous jungle of the Bataan Peninsula, the northern arm of Manila Bay. There, and in the coast-defense complex at the bay mouth—Corregidor and Forts Drum, Frank, and Hughes on smaller islands—he would fight a delaying action until the U.S. Pacific Fleet rushed westward to his aid.

The Japanese plan was comparatively simple. Lieutenant General Masaharu Homma's 14th Army was scheduled to subdue MacArthur's forces on Luzon and secure the island in fifty days. His army—made up of the 16th and 48th Divisions, together with support and service units—totaled about fifty thousand veteran troops. Homma expected MacArthur's half-trained and ill-equipped, mostly Filipino forces to offer little resistance. After a rapid conquest of Luzon, the 48th Division would then move on to further operations in the south, assuming all went well.

In practice, neither MacArthur's defensive strategy nor Homma's offensive timetable played out well.

The First Month

In the first two days of the war, Japanese planes launched an all-out assault on northern and southern Luzon. Their aerial onslaughts devastated the naval base at Cavite, on the south side of Manila Bay, destroying everything in their paths—ships, installations, stores, and munitions. Homma initiated preliminary landings at Aparri and Vigan in the north and at Legazpi in the south. His air support groups established air bases in the north and shuttled in aircraft from Formosa.

At this time, Brereton transferred the remnants of the American air forces to Mindanao, and the Navy Department ordered all that was left of the Asiatic Fleet to Java. Only four destroyers, the submarines, a flotilla of PT boats, and a squadron of fly-ing boats—along with a regiment of marines—remained in the Philippines.

To MacArthur's credit, he would not allow Homma's first landings to divert his attention from Lingayen Gulf, the site of the anticipated *real* invasion yet to come. He told reporters that he could not defend every beach. "The basic principle in handling my troops," he explained, "is to hold them intact until the enemy commits himself in force."[25]

At that point MacArthur's thinking was sound. It faltered when he persisted in the belief that his unseasoned troops were up to the task of hurling a veteran invader

The naval base at Cavite after the attack by Japanese planes. The bombing destroyed ships, installations, and vital medical supplies and food.

back into the sea. Having rejected War Plan Orange-3 as "stereotyped" and "defeatist,"[26] he could not bring himself to reactivate WPO-3 until faced with no other choice. Only pure vanity, it seems, kept MacArthur from retiring his forces into the more defensible mountainous jungles of the Bataan Peninsula *without waiting* for Homma to strike Luzon in force.

Homma's main force, veterans of the China war, began landing operations at Lingayen Gulf on 22 December at 0200. By dawn they had established three beachheads ashore. Green Filipino troops at two invasion points dropped their heavy Enfield rifles and fled. At Rosario, twenty miles south of their beachhead, the invaders overcame light resistance in a brief pitched battle. Under an umbrella of fighter planes from newly established bases in northern Luzon, they quickly linked up with Japanese troops from the Vigan beachhead. By afternoon they were barreling down Route 3, the cobblestoned military highway leading to Manila.

Meanwhile, additional Japanese troops had gained a toehold on Mindanao, while the island's Filipino defenders faded off into the hills. The island of Jolo fell on 25 December. These quick conquests enabled the Japanese to set up air and naval bases for further operations against the Dutch East Indies.

Back on Luzon, Homma's invaders, driving the partially trained Filipino troops before them, advanced rapidly southward. Wainwright withdrew in five successive

Lieutenant General Homma (center) comes ashore at Luzon as his main assault force advances on the island toward Manila.

moves, saved from disaster only by the gallantry and dependability of a few American and Philippine Scout units. While MacArthur weighed a request from Wainwright to withdraw behind the Agno River, he received word from Parker's South Luzon Force that the Japanese had landed a second formidable force at Lamon Bay, sixty miles southeast of Manila.

Until then, MacArthur had vacillated. Now, a glance at the map clearly indicated that a giant enemy pincer movement was in the making. Only fast action would save his command from extinction in the closing enemy claw. On Christmas Day he radioed all his commanders: "WPO is in effect."[27]

The next day, with three columns of some seven thousand Japanese troops already advancing northward toward Manila from Lamon Bay, he proclaimed: "In order to spare Manila from any possible air or ground attacks, consideration is being given by military authorities to declaring Manila an open city, as was done in the case of Paris, Brussels, and Rome during this war."[28] (An open city is one declared unoccupied by defending forces to spare it from needless destruction by attacking forces.) MacArthur's proclamation took effect two days later.

During the next week, Philippine Army units, supported by U.S. regulars, counterattacked the vanguard of Homma's forces. Their rally delayed Homma's spearhead long enough to allow Parker's South Luzon Force to withdraw across the Calumpit Bridge spanning the unfordable Pampanga River and into the Bataan Peninsula. Wainwright's North Luzon Force temporarily stonewalled Homma's southward advance at Plaridel, ten miles northeast of the bridge, then followed the U.S. southern force into the peninsula, blowing up the bridge behind them. By 6 January 1942, all of MacArthur's forces—some eighty thousand American and Filipino troops—were safe on the Bataan side of the river, having skillfully executed a precisely coordinated withdrawal.

Bataan: First Defense Line

MacArthur began his defense of the peninsula with his forces astride the mountainous jungle at its base. Wainwright's I Corps deployed to the west and Parker's II Corps to the east, bracketing the near-impassable Mount Natib in the middle. MacArthur opted to defend the mountain's vine- and jungle-covered slopes only by patrols. The Americans called this the Abucay Line, as it stretched across the neck of the peninsula from Abucay in the east to Mauban in the west.

In little more than a week after MacArthur's decision to implement WPO-3, the Americans had moved vast stores of ammunition into Bataan. But since top priority had been given to military supplies, they had laid in only about a month's supply of food. MacArthur's staff worried even more about the shortage of medical supplies, especially quinine, as malaria posed an ever-present danger in the region. And to worsen the problem, an influx of at least twenty-six thousand civilian refugees had crowded into Bataan, adding a further drain on the already short provisions. MacArthur immediately placed everyone on half-rations. Militarily, the move into the peninsula had enhanced MacArthur's position. Logistically, his situation in everything except ammunition was precarious at best.

MacArthur—accompanied by his staff and Manuel Quezon, president of the Philippines—now moved to Corregidor, two miles off the tip of the peninsula. He established his headquarters in Malinta

MacArthur's headquarters on Corregidor were inside the Malinta Tunnel (pictured).

Tunnel, a central tunnel carved out of rock, with side passages for hospital wards. His wife, Jean, and his son, Arthur, had been ferried out to the island from Manila a few days earlier. The presence of the MacArthurs provided a source of inspiration to the island's defenders in the days ahead, Colonel Clear wrote later:

> All through the endless days of hardship and horror, General MacArthur's courage and coolness contributed to the maintenance of morale throughout all ranks. The same is to be said for Mrs. MacArthur. Many a night she had to make a dash from the exposed frame house in which she slept to the shelter of the tunnel, carrying little Arthur, their son, in her arms. Arthur never came willingly—he wanted to see the bombs burst.[29]

Until his departure, MacArthur would direct the peninsula defenses from this island fortress known formally as Fort Mills and less formally as "The Rock." He often exhorted his troops to fight on for "help is on the way from the United States—thousands of troops and hundreds of planes are being dispatched."[30] They were not, of course, because they were not yet available. But the general did not know this at the time.

After Japanese forces occupied Manila on 2 January, General Homma received orders to ship his 48th Division to Java. The 48th, once the heart of his army, was to be replaced by the 65th Brigade, under Lieutenant General Akira Nara. The brigade of about seventy-five hundred occupation troops comprised mostly older men, ill equipped and almost totally unprepared for frontline combat. On 10 January, two columns of the 65th snaked their way down the peninsula, one to the east, the other to the west side of Mount Natib.

At 1530, Parker's artillery opened up on Nara's eastern column as it passed through sugarcane fields about twenty miles north of Mariveles. Wainwright's I Corps engaged Nara's western column before nightfall. Outnumbered and without air and artillery support, Nara's brigade struck again and again at the Abucay Line for the next twelve days, only to be repulsed repeatedly by its defenders. Meanwhile, however, a regimental-sized Japanese task force was probing the center of the defense line and eventually discovered an avenue across the ostensibly impenetrable Mount Natib.

On the night of 21 January, General Nara called on Colonel Takeo Imai's 141st Infantry Regiment, already decimated by constant attacks, to launch an all-out assault on the now-disintegrating American-Filipino left flank. "You are to drive the enemy southeastward," Nara told Imai, "and annihilate them."[31] At noon on the 22nd, Imai's troops burst out of the jungle to the rear of the Abucay Line and threatened to split MacArthur's defenses. MacArthur ordered an immediate withdrawal to a more easily defended fallback position along the Bagac-Orion Line, about fifteen miles from the tip of the peninsula. MacArthur wired George C. Marshall, the army chief of staff in Washington, promising that his forces would "fight it out to complete destruction."[32]

Bataan: Second Defense Line

While MacArthur's forces continued to meet and hurl back one vicious assault after another on the new defense line—and against Mount Samat, an extinct volcano at its center—Homma decided to try a different tactic. On 23 January, he landed a small amphibious force well behind American lines on the seaward side of the peninsula, followed three days later by a battalion-sized force. American and Filipino rear-echelon troops engaged and contained them. After two-plus weeks of fierce fighting (29 January–13 February), the defenders, aided by harassing PT boats and artillery from Corregidor's big guns, repulsed the invaders. By then, Homma had already called off his attacks against Mount Samat on 8 February.

Homma now paused to assess his situation. His forces, reduced drastically by the loss of the 48th Division and battle casualties—seven thousand dead and wounded plus some ten thousand victims of disease—now stood at three thousand able-bodied troops. An American counterattack, he feared, could bring disaster upon him and his skeleton force. Homma felt compelled to appeal to Tokyo for reinforcements, fully realizing that his appeal meant the end of his military career. Battlefield activity fell into an eerie lull while Homma waited for help to arrive from Japan.

MacArthur at first welcomed the lull, interpreting it as a victory in which his beloved troops had stopped the Japanese in their tracks. American reporters now lauded Bataan's defenders as great heroes and elevated MacArthur to a godlike status, boosting morale in the United States at the same time it began to falter in the Philippines. Weeks of short rations had taken their toll. Malnutrition set in, and with it a bevy of diseases, such as beriberi, dysentery, and malaria. Medical officers declared some sixty thousand soldiers unfit for duty by mid-March. And the hungry grew hungrier.

Cooks butchered everything edible that they could lay their hands on—water buffalo, pack mules, polo ponies, and cavalry horses, and even an occasional giant python. One nurse later recalled, "When a water buffalo was roasted, it was not so bad . . . but when it was stewed, Heaven was not too high for the odor."[33] Still, daily rations dwindled to about one thousand calories a day, about one-quarter of what young men in combat need to sustain themselves.

When the days droned on with no help arriving or even in view, a scathing verse began circulating in the ranks:

We're the battling bastards of Bataan:
No mama, no papa, no Uncle Sam,
No aunts, no uncles, no nephews, no nieces,
No rifles, no planes, no artillery pieces,
And nobody gives a damn.[34]

And more than a few uncomplimentary poems featuring "Dugout Doug Mac-

MacArthur on Strategy

In "Disaster—and Glory—in the Philippines," published in the *Reader's Digest Illustrated Story of World War II*, General Douglas MacArthur reflects on his defense of the Philippines:

> To allow my main bodies to be compressed into the central plain in defense of Manila by an enemy advancing from both directions could only mean early and complete destruction. By retiring into the peninsula, I could exploit maneuverability of my full forces to the limit and gain our only chance of survival. Our plan of defense, therefore, was that [Major General Jonathan M.] Wainwright would fight a delaying action on successive lines across the great central plain from Lingayen Gulf on the north to the neck of the Bataan Peninsula in the south. Under cover of these delaying actions [Brigadeer General Albert M.] Jones with his troops from Manila and the central plain would all be withdrawn into Bataan, where I could pit my own intimate knowledge of the terrain against the Japanese superiority in air power, tanks, artillery, and men.
>
> The Japanese had not expected that our forces would be withdrawn from Manila, intending to fight the decisive battle of the campaign for control of the city. . . . Our tenacious defense against tremendous odds completely upset the Japanese military timetable, and enabled the Allies to gain precious months for the organization of the defense of Australia and the vital eastern areas of the Southwest Pacific.

Arthur" made the rounds, chastising him for not informing President Roosevelt of the troops' plight in the Philippines. In truth, however, he had done his utmost in this regard. But Washington had already mentally written off the fate of MacArthur's defense force.

On 21 February, Roosevelt sent MacArthur a direct order to evacuate Corregidor. The general objected strenuously to the president's command but in the end complied, hoping to garner reinforcements and return to the Philippines.

In a last meeting with Wainwright, whom he left in command, MacArthur promised to return. "If you're still on Bataan when I get back," he said, shaking hands with Wainwright, "I'll make you a lieutenant general." "I'll be on Bataan if I'm alive,"[35] Wainwright replied.

On the evening of 11 March, MacArthur, with his family and a small party of aides, sped out of Corregidor on a PT boat to Mindanao and from there, via B-17, left for Darwin, Australia.

Fall of Bataan

On 3 April, General Masaharu Homma's army, now ballooned to fifty thousand by reinforcements, and in company with dominating air and artillery support, resumed their attacks on the Bagac-Orion Line. Following a massive artillery barrage on the lower slopes of Mount Samat, Japanese bombers dropped incendiary bombs on the cane fields and scorched American positions. Homma's fresh troops tore a wide gap in the left flank of II Corps, and the attackers surged through en masse, driving Parker's troops back ten miles in forty-eight hours. In the west, I Corps, now commanded by Brigadier General Albert M. Jones, folded back toward the sea. Jones attempted counterattacks, but the enemy repulsed them handily. After five days of desperate fighting, II Corps disintegrated, virtually wiped out to the last man.

On the evening of 8 April, Major General Edward P. King Jr., successor to Wainwright as commander of all forces on Bataan, told his staff, "I have decided to surrender Bataan. I have not communicated with General Wainwright because I do not want him to assume any part of the responsibility."[36] At 0900 the next morning, while driving toward the front to meet with Homma's deputies, the thought occurred to King that Lee had surrendered to Grant at Appomattox on that same day, 9 April, long ago.

Without Wainwright's knowledge, King had surrendered seventy-six thousand troops, including twelve thousand Americans, because it was the merciful thing to do. Bataan's emaciated and diseased defenders became the largest American army in history to lay down its arms. Americans will always honor them not for how the battle ended but for how they fought.

After the fall of Bataan, the Japanese treated members of the Philippine Army with unexpected kindness, permitting many of them to return to their homes. Such was hardly the case with Filipino and American regulars. Their Japanese captors quickly herded them off to San Fernando, sixty-five miles up the Bataan Peninsula.

Retirement to Bataan

In "Retreat to Bataan," an excerpt appearing in *The War, 1939–1945,* (edited by Desmond Flower and James Reeves), William Martin Camp, a marine participant, describes the fighting withdrawal to the Bataan Peninsula:

"To the rear! To the rear!"

From Lingayen to the tar-covered Olongapo Road, then to Abucay, farther down Bataan. Infantry, artillery, cavalry, and machine-gun units tried to hold them [the Japanese] back, but they just kept coming, all the way, head on, at point-blank range. There was nothing to stop them. They came in by the hundreds, the thousands. Their blood ran down the hills, seeped into the earth until it was sticky, then ran over the surface like water, down the valleys and into the streams, and down the streams into the sea. Bodies cascaded down the hills like waterfalls, rolling and tumbling and lying still. Others followed, and the command was always:

"To the rear . . . to the rear! . . ."

The Filipino Scouts held them off for the first eleven days and eleven nights after the Lingayen invasion. It was continuous attacking, retreating to new positions, stopping long enough to slaughter a few hundred more, then being driven back by the overwhelming numbers. There weren't enough guns to stop them. . . .

This was the retirement to Bataan.

Japanese soldiers (pictured) continue their advance as American and Filipino troops withdraw to Bataan.

Deprived of food and water, beaten, and sometimes murdered, some 7,000 to 10,000 prisoners died along the way, during what is now called the Bataan Death March. Included among the dead were 2,330 Americans. Those who survived the sixty-five-mile trek were shipped by freight wagon to Camp O'Donnell, beyond Clark Field. For presiding over such atrocities in the Philippines, General Homma was tried as a war criminal after the war and hanged.

"Ghastly Men, Still Unafraid"

After Bataan capitulated, Corregidor's defenders could see their own fate clearly, but they continued to hold out. General

Homma, ever the cautious commander, did not attempt to land an invasion force on The Rock immediately. Instead, for the next four weeks, he blasted the island fortress and its three island satellites with the full force of his aircraft and artillery from Bataan and Cavite. "Day after day the enemy batteries on Bataan poured their screaming projectiles into the [Malinta] tunnel mouth," Colonel Clear wrote later, "tearing away the face of the cliffs, smothering the beach defenders in bloody debris."[37]

On 4 May alone, some sixteen thousand shells burst on The Rock while General Homma prepared to launch an invasion force from the port of Lamao at the tip of the Bataan Peninsula. That night, preceded

After surrendering on Bataan, American troops are forced to pose with their captors for a Japanese propaganda photograph.

by another fierce barrage, fifty two Japanese landing craft churned toward Corregidor bearing two thousand assault troops. Driven off course by the swift currents of Manila Bay, they missed their intended landing beaches by a mile or more. When the boats tried to land, cannoneers of the 1st Marine Battalion, taking advantage of a rising moon, blasted thirty-one of them out of the water. Still, some six hundred invaders managed to scramble ashore and seize control of the eastern end of the island.

While the enemy established a beachhead on his island, General Wainwright received a special radio message from President Roosevelt: "You and your devoted followers have become the symbols of our war effort and the guarantee of our victory."[38] A later local message informed him that Japanese attackers had overrun the marine battery.

In the predawn light, marines of Headquarters and Service Company, along with five hundred untrained sailors, staged a counterattack. They caught the invaders—who had paused to await air and tank support—by surprise and drove them back on both flanks. By 1000, however, the Americans could hear the ominous clank and rumble of approaching tanks and were forced to withdraw.

Wainwright, defenseless against tanks, needed little imagination to envisage the carnage that they would surely visit upon the sick,

The remaining defenders of the Philippines surrender at the entrance to the Malinta Tunnel. MacArthur swore to avenge the sacrifices made by those he was forced to leave behind.

passed. Without prospect of relief I feel it is my duty to my country and to my gallant troops to end this useless effusion of blood and human sacrifice.[39]

At midnight on 6–7 May, Wainwright, reduced to a three-day water supply, agreed to a ceasefire with Homma and called for the surrender of all American troops in the Philippines. Most Americans complied, but pockets of guerrilla activity continued throughout the rest of the war. In Australia, General MacArthur, now commander of the Southwest Pacific Area, told the press:

starving, and wounded sheltered in the Malinta Tunnel. He knew what he had to do. In a last radio message to President Roosevelt, he announced his intention to surrender his thirteen-thousand-troop command, "but not in shame." In part, he said:

There is a limit of human endurance and that limit has long since been

Corregidor needs no comment from me. It has sounded its own story at the mouth of its guns. It has scrolled its own epitaph on enemy tablets. But through the bloody haze of its last reverberating shot, I shall always seem to see a vision of grim, gaunt, ghastly men, still unafraid.[40]

Perhaps it was that searing vision of those "ghastly men" that drove him to avenge their sacrifices and deaths. In any event, it was at MacArthur's insistence and through his perseverance that the Second Battle of the Philippines was fought in 1944–1945—and *won*—by his forces.

Chapter 3

Guadalcanal:
The First U.S.
Offensive

"Guadalcanal was like a bald-headed guy. There might be hair on the side of the head, but the top was bare. The ridges were bare, but below was deep vegetation, a deep gorge and the jungle."

—Donald Moss, USMC (quoted in
Eric Bergerud, *Touched with Fire*)

"Attention on deck!"* blared an impersonal voice over the ships' loudspeakers in the pale gray light of dawn on 7 August 1942. *"Marines report to your debark stations!"*

Fifty ships of U.S. Task Force 61, bearing some nineteen thousand men of the 1st Marine Division, steamed into Savo Sound and lay off Guadalcanal and Florida Island in the Solomon Island chain. Combat-equipped troops of the 1st Battalion, 5th Marines, clad in mottled-green camouflaged utilities and helmets and distinctive canvas leggings, assembled at their stations in orderly haste.

"Away all boats!" barked the amplified voice. Down went the landing craft. Moments later came the command that every-

one awaited with butterflies of apprehension: *"Land the landing force!"* Marines of the first wave clambered down cargo nets splayed over the side of the transports and dropped into the boats bobbing alongside.

After planes from the U.S. aircraft carriers *Saratoga, Wasp,* and *Enterprise* outlined the limits of the landing zone with colored smoke, the white-tailed flotilla of invasion craft set out for shore. Meanwhile, three heavy cruisers, *Quincy, Vincennes,* and *Astoria,* and four destroyers laced the sixteen-hundred-yard strip of black sand and the jungle behind it with a blanket of five- and eight-inch shells.

At 0910, the landing craft scudded ashore. The marines scrambled over the sides of their boats and waded through a

As marines climb down a cargo net into their landing craft, another boat begins its run toward the beach at Guadalcanal.

moderate surf to the beach, weapons upraised. A few minutes later, a red flare signaled to the invasion fleet offshore that the marines had landed without resistance. But the battle for Guadalcanal—the first Amer-

ican offensive land action in the Pacific—had only just begun.

Operation Watchtower

Less than two months after the humiliating American defeat in the Philippines, news of the dramatic U.S. naval victory at Midway (4–7 June 1942) boosted the spirits of a downcast nation just when the national mood most needed something positive and uplifting. With Midway now secure, the U.S. Joint Chiefs of Staff (JCS) looked with growing optimism at their options for launching limited offensive operations in the Pacific. Interservice rivalries, chance, and not least the acute vision of Admiral Ernest J. King, the commander in chief of the U.S. Fleet (COMINCH), each played a key role in deciding the Allies' first offensive objective west of Midway. The Joint Chiefs soon focused their attention on New Guinea and the Solomon Islands in the Southwest Pacific Area, General Douglas MacArthur's domain.

MacArthur, hoping to gain command of the entire Pacific Theater, demanded a marine division and two carrier task forces to implement his grandiose offensive scheme called "Tulsa." The general proposed a lightning campaign in New Guinea, calling for the capture of Rabaul—Japan's main base in the South Pacific—in less than three weeks and "forcing the enemy back 700 miles to his base at Truk."[41] Admiral King—tough, rapier witted, and short fused—also recognized the chance to seize the initiative in the South Pacific.

"Since the Japanese had gotten a rude shock [decisive defeat] at Midway," he noted later, "here was a good chance to get the enemy off balance and *keep* him off balance."[42] King and the navy agreed that Rabaul should be taken. But the crusty, sixty-three-year-old admiral was not about to commit two of his precious carriers to the poorly charted waters of the Solomon Sea, within range of land-based Japanese aircraft. He also was not eager to assist MacArthur—whom he considered a supreme egotist and grandstander—in any operation that might dilute the navy's command authority over most of the Pacific. King proposed an alternate plan.

Operation Watchtower, as King's plan came to be known, favored a gradual advance on the Japanese bastion at Rabaul through New Guinea *and* the Solomons. Since it would be an amphibious operation, King insisted that Admiral Chester W. Nimitz—and *not* MacArthur—should preside over it. After a week of robust arguments, the JCS agreed to King's proposal, in principle, but divided it into three separate offensives, or "tasks."

Task One, with Nimitz in overall command, called for the occupation of the Santa Cruz Islands, preparatory to an attack against Tulagi—the Japanese mid-Solomons base across from Guadalcanal—no later than 1 August. In Task Two, MacArthur was

Admiral Ernest J. King (top) proposed the amphibious operation against the Solomon Islands with Admiral Chester W. Nimitz (bottom) in charge.

to direct an advance along the northeast coast of New Guinea, parallel with an island-hopping advance up the central Solomons overseen by Nimitz. Task Three would close the Allied pincers with a two-pronged assault on New Britain and Rabaul. To avert confusion or further bickering over command jurisdiction, the Joint Chiefs cleverly shifted the boundaries of Nimitz's South Pacific Area to the west of Guadalcanal, thereby bringing the Solomons under U.S. Navy control. Guadalcanal itself did not figure in this early version of Operation Watchtower. Then chance took a hand.

Early in July, American cryptanalysts (code-breakers) and radio-traffic analysts reported enemy preparations for a major new offensive in the Southwest Pacific. Word of a new Japanese airfield nearing completion on Guadalcanal sounded a general alert. The Japanese, it seemed, also coveted the New Guinea–Solomons region. With control of the Solomons, the gate would spring open to them for easy conquests of the New Hebrides, New Caledonia, the Fijis, and New Zealand. In this event, the Japanese would cut the lifeline from America to Australia and New Zealand, a development not relished by the Joint Chiefs. The JCS hastily revised Operation Watchtower to target Guadalcanal as its primary objective, hurriedly working out change details in only a week and setting D day (the date for launching the operation) as 7 August.

D Day at Guadalcanal and Tulagi

As commander of the South Pacific Area, Vice Admiral Robert L. Ghormley assumed overall responsibility for Operation Watchtower. Frank Jack Fletcher, newly promoted to vice admiral for his role in the stunning U.S. victory at Midway, was appointed commander of Task Force (TF) 61—*Saratoga, Wasp,* and *Enterprise,* the new battleship *North Carolina,* and six cruisers. Rear Admiral Richmond Kelly Turner, the recently departed head of King's War Plans Division, took command of Task Force 62 (the amphibious force). Major General Alexander A. Vandegrift, a veteran of jungle campaigning in Nicaragua, commanded the marines. Task Force 44—five American and three Australian cruisers, plus fifteen destroyers—was assigned to cover the landings, with the Royal Navy's Rear Admiral Victor A. C. Crutchley commanding.

Vandegrift's 1st Marine Division consisted of men who had been training together for almost a year and of raw hands fresh from boot camp, the latter element added late to bring the division up to combat strength. Old and obsolete fairly described much of their equipment as the untested leathernecks headed toward the Solomons. Moreover, intelligence about the island chain fell short of adequate. And what few charts of the region were available dated back to the turn of the century and left much to the imagination. The official Marine Corps history assesses the preinvasion situation tersely and precisely: "Seldom has an operation been begun under more disadvantageous circumstances."[43] The task forces assembled in the Fijis and left there at dusk on 31 July.

The Solomons—the destination of this hastily put together aggregation of ships and men—stretch southeasterly from the tip of New Guinea in two chains toward

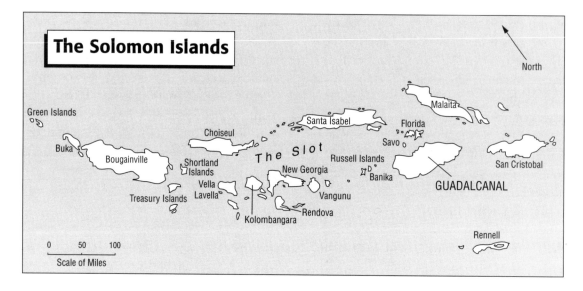

New Caledonia, the Fijis, and Samoa. Anchored in the north by Bougainville, about five degrees below the equator, the Solomons' double chain extends for about six hundred miles. A wide channel known as the Slot separates the parallel strings of several large islands and innumerable small ones. Guadalcanal, ninety-two miles long and thirty-three miles wide, dominates the archipelago. Across from Malaita to the east, it forms a rough arrowhead of the Indispensable Strait pointing toward New Caledonia and beyond.

On 6 August, Admiral Fletcher's Task Force 61 detached itself from the rest of the invasion fleet about sixty miles south of Guadalcanal and remained in open waters. That evening Admiral Turner's TF 62 steamed north and rounded Cape Esperance, the northwestern point of Guadalcanal, and entered Sealark Channel. The channel separates Guadalcanal from Savo

Island, a sheer volcanic cone that rises starkly out of the water and stands sentinel-like at the channel's mouth.

As the ships of TF 62 slogged around Cape Esperance, the island's offshore smell assailed even the most insensitive noses of marines who had come topside seeking relief from the sweltering August heat. The pungent odor of rotting vegetation was an aroma that many of them would come to associate with death in the days ahead. It seemed to heighten the tenseness that every man felt. Richard Tregaskis, a twenty-six-year-old correspondent on his first combat assignment, reported:

Everyone seemed ready to jump at the first boom of a gun, but there was little excitement. The thing that was happening was so unbelievable that it seemed like a dream. We were slipping through the narrow neck of water between Guadalcanal and Savo Islands; we were practically inside Tulagi Bay, almost past the Jap shore batteries, and not a shot had been fired.[44]

About five miles east of Savo, TF 62 divided into two groups. One group headed for Lunga Point on the "Canal," as marines came to know the larger island; the other headed for Tulagi across the channel.

At first light, marines of Colonel Merritt A. Edson's 1st Raider Battalion stormed ashore on Tulagi, marking the first American assault landing since 1898. The Japanese commander, appalled at the size of the marine landing force, radioed Rabaul: "Enemy troop strength is overwhelming. We will fight to the last man."[45] And so they did. But "Red Mike" Edson's raiders cleared the island in three days.

Across the way at Lunga Point, marines of the 1st and 3rd Battalions, 5th Marines, landed almost unopposed on Red Beach, just east of the Tenaru River. They advanced southwest to the airfield (later named Henderson Field in honor of Lofton Henderson, a marine pilot killed at Midway). The marines reached the airstrip, key to Japanese plans for taking Port Moresby, toward the end of the second day. To their surprise, they found the landing strip—3,778 feet long by 160 feet wide—undefended. The Japanese had fled inland. (Marine intelligence learned later that the entire Japanese force on the island when the marines landed numbered only about two thousand, mostly Korean laborers who were guarded and supervised by some six hundred troops.) The marines immediately set up a defense system along the east bank of the Tenaru River to the east of the airstrip and on a grassy ridge two miles shy of the Mataniko River to the west.

Meanwhile, on Red Beach, an undermanned shore party struggled to offload precious stores and munitions. Three prompt and violent enemy air attacks at midday reminded them of their opposition

Marines land almost unopposed at Lunga Point soon after daybreak. The small force of Japanese defenders had fled inland.

and played havoc with their efforts. Chaos ruled over their unloading activities, resulting in an abortive exercise that they would later greatly regret. By nightfall on D day, the marines had successfully landed eleven thousand men on Guadalcanal but not nearly enough supplies to sustain them in the days to come.

"Our Necks Were Out"

The importance of logistics to any military operation can never be overstated, as the marines ashore soon learned. To worsen their situation of underprovisioning, Japanese headquarters in Rabaul sent a naval flotilla of seven cruisers and one destroyer rushing southward under Vice Admiral Gunichi Mikawa. In the meantime, Japanese aircraft continued to attack the next day, and a series of air battles developed over the Slot. American carrier planes took a heavy toll on the attackers but lost 20 percent of their own aircraft. Admiral Fletcher, fearing that the reduction of air cover had left his carriers vulnerable, radioed Admiral Ghormley:

Fighter strength reduced from 99 to 78. In view of large numbers of enemy torpedo planes and bombers in this area, I recommend the immediate withdrawal of my carriers. Request tankers be sent forward immediately as fuel is running low.[46]

Without waiting for confirmation, Fletcher withdrew and set course for home. By 2100

that night, TF 61 was well beyond reach of Guadalcanal.

Samuel Eliot Morison, dean of U.S. naval historians, later observed that Fletcher's remaining seventy-eight fighters were still more than he had commanded at Midway, that his ships had adequate fuel for several more days, and that "his force could have remained in the area with no more consequences than sunburn."[47]

Heat from a different source struck Turner's escort squadron shortly after midnight on 9 August. Admiral Mikawa's cruiser-destroyer force slipped past Savo Is-

The USS Enterprise *cruises south of Guadalcanal. Fearing that a reduction in air cover left his carriers vulnerable, Admiral Fletcher withdrew them from action.*

land into the Slot and surprised Admiral Crutchley's Task Force 44. In a violent thirty-minute night action, Mikawa sank four Allied cruisers in the Battle of Savo Island. "We took a hell of a beating,"[48] Admiral Turner wrote later. It was the worst sea defeat in the entire history of the U.S. Navy.

Fortunately for Turner's transport and cargo ships, which might have been caught still offloading, Mikawa turned around abruptly after his swift victory and sped for home. His failure to exploit his triumph at the expense of Turner's sitting-duck landing ships was only one of many opportunities missed by the Japanese during the Guadalcanal campaign.

Fletcher's departure, a day earlier than originally scheduled, had left Admiral Turner livid with rage. Without the formidable protection of TF 61's air umbrella, he felt obligated to withdraw his own task force. Nonetheless, despite Mikawa's intrusion off Savo, Turner remained on station for another day, putting ashore as many more stores as possible in the space of twenty-four hours. Even so, when Task Force 62 weighed anchor at dawn on 9 August, it was still carrying one thousand of the marine division's reserve troops, most of its equipment and heavy artillery, and approximately half its food supplies.

Vandegrift's marines felt isolated and abandoned. The general told his officers to brief them on their situation, withholding nothing. "But," he added, "pound home to them that we anticipate no Bataan, no Wake Island."[49]

At the bottom of the military pecking order, one marine private was not entirely convinced. He later explained, "I figured it this way: Our necks were out, and it was just a question of how far down the Japs were going to chop."[50]

Battle of Tenaru River

Unknown to the marines at this time, the Japanese were hardly in a position to do much chopping. Their regional commanders in Rabaul were preoccupied with their invasion of Papua, one thousand miles to the west. Moreover, they did not have land reinforcements available for countering an American threat to Guadalcanal—one that they had yet to accept as serious. They felt confident that their naval and air forces could cut the marines' supply line and contain them until a five-thousand-man detachment of Lieutenant General Harukichi Hyakutake's 17th Army arrived from Guam in about ten days. In the meantime, the marines on Guadalcanal spent the first two weeks attempting to clean out annoying pockets of the enemy—experienced, elusive jungle fighters—in the region just west of the brown-flowing Mataniko River.

On 20 August, the arrival of thirty-one Marine Corps aircraft (twelve Dauntless dive-bombers and nineteen Wildcat fighters) provided the marines with striking power and lessened their feelings of isolation. The marines promptly dubbed the new arrivals the "Cactus Air Force," after the code name for Guadalcanal. General Vandegrift, upon viewing the dive-bombers,

At the end of its dive, a Dauntless releases its bomb. Together with Wildcat fighters, Dauntlesses of the "Cactus Air Force" provided the marines with much-needed air cover and striking power.

Urged forward by sword-wielding officers screaming banzais, Ichiki's troops charged ahead with bayonets fixed and rifles cracking. Some tossed powerful firecrackers for shock effect. Robert Leckie, a noted military historian and former marine who fought in the battle that followed, later described how it began:

Everyone was firing, every weapon was sounding voice; but this was no orchestration, no terribly beautiful symphony of death, as decadent rear-echelon observers write. Here was cacophony; here was dissonance; here was wildness; here was the absence of rhythm, the loss of limit, for everyone fires what, when and where he chooses; here was booming, sounding, shrieking, wailing, hissing, crashing, shaking, gibbering noise. Here was hell.[52]

called it "one of the most beautiful sights of my life."[51] Marine air strength on the Canal eventually totaled about one hundred aircraft.

That same night (20–21 August), five hundred men of a Japanese special landing force—an advance element of the 17th Army from Guam under Colonel Kiyono Ichiki—infiltrated through a coconut plantation just to the east of the marine perimeter. At 0120 they burst out of the trees and charged toward the marines across a sandspit at the mouth of the Tenaru River.

The Japanese piled up against a single strand of barbed wire, and a blizzard of marine rifle and machine-gun fire chopped them down. Some broke through the perimeter, and the marines fought them off with knives and bayonets. The marines held on through the night and counterattacked at dawn.

Dauntless dive-bombers from newly completed Henderson Field bombed and strafed the coconut grove again and again. Marine tanks rolled into the grove afterward and crushed the Japanese troops left alive beneath their tracks. Vandegrift noted, "The rear of the tanks looked like meat grinders."[53] When the fighting ended, six hundred Japanese lay dead. Marine dead totaled thirty-five in their first major action.

Marine Corps maps incorrectly marked the Ilu River as the Tenaru. But to marines—past, present, and future—the action on the Ilu will always be called the Battle of Tenaru River. "From that time on," declared Samuel Eliot Morison, "United States Marines were invincible."[54]

After the Battle of Tenaru River, marines used tanks to crush the Japanese troops who survived the American counterattack.

War at Sea

The battle at the Ilu finally convinced the Japanese command in Rabaul that substantial reinforcements must be diverted to Guadalcanal. The American command was also aware that the 1st Marine Division would need help to retain its precarious beachhead. Guadalcanal became a giant funnel in the Southwest Pacific into which both sides poured all of their available men and resources, setting the stage for a great battle of attrition.

For the next three weeks, sporadic encounters between American and Japanese patrols increased in frequency and intensity. During the day, American aircraft dominated the skies and U.S. Navy warships ruled the waters in the Tulagi-Guadalcanal region.

But after dark, Japanese destroyers and cruisers raced down the Slot to land troops and supplies on Guadalcanal and to bombard marine positions and Henderson Field. The marines dubbed these nightly conveyers of shell, troops, and stores the "Tokyo Express."

Attempts by both sides to interfere with each other's supply lines touched off a string of intricate air and naval battles between 22 August and 30 November. Some of them, such as the Battle of the Eastern Solomons (22–25 August) and the Battle of the Santa Cruz Islands (26–27 October), were long-range aerial duels fought between opposing carrier aircraft. Others, like the Battle of Cape Esperance (11–13 October), the Naval Battle of Guadalcanal (12–15 November), and the Battle of Tassafaronga (30 November), were fought at night between surface vessels at thunderously close range.

Admiral Turner called the Naval Battle of Guadalcanal "the fiercest naval battle ever fought."[55] A British naval captain later pointed out that the Americans fought as many sea battles around Guadalcanal as the Royal Navy had fought in the whole of World War I. Overall, losses on both sides about evened out, but the strategic advantage went to the Americans. They could replace their losses. The Japanese, lacking in vital resources, could not.

Battle of Bloody Ridge

The next and perhaps greatest test for Vandegrift's marines came between 12 and 14 September. On the night of the 12th, following intensive naval shelling of a sector of the marine perimeter later known as Bloody Ridge, factions of General Hyakutake's 17th Army attacked in force. Colonel Red Mike Edson's 1st Raider Battalion, moved over from Tulagi, was dug in at the base of the ridge, south of Henderson Field. After three days of the bitterest fighting the raiders—and all other available marines—had seen so far, they repulsed the attackers. The battle claimed 600 Japanese dead and another 500 wounded. Marines took losses of 260 dead or wounded. Marine combat correspondent Frank Hough, in his account of the battle, points out:

> What made Bloody Ridge, and the Guadalcanal campaign in general, such a terrible experience was the unending pressure to which all hands were subjected. There were no rest areas or recreation facilities, nowhere a man could go and nothing he could do to recuperate nerves rubbed raw by the strain of what amounted to perpetual combat. There was scarcely a day or night during the four months the 1st Marine Division was on Guadalcanal when it was not attacking or being attacked by land, sea or air, and in many instances all three.[56]

Moreover, as Hough goes on to note, the marines were shock troops, neither trained nor equipped to fight defensively for long periods. Added to that, much of their equipment had been hauled away upon the premature departure of Task Force 62. And help did not arrive until mid-October, when an army regiment landed to reinforce—but not replace—them.

The Sendai Offensive

Over the next month, while violent air and sea battles raged over and around Guadalcanal, both sides continued to build up their forces. On 18 September, the 7th Marine Regiment, the final element of the 1st Marine Division, arrived on the island. Lieutenant General Harukichi Hyakutake, commander of the 17th Army, landed with most of his 2nd Division on 9 October. His forces now numbered about twenty thousand. The 2nd Division included a squadron of medium tanks and a regiment of 150-millimeter howitzers, which soon began shelling the marine beachhead. The U.S. 164th Infantry Regiment, the first army reinforcements, came ashore on 13 October. Vandegrift's forces now totaled about twenty-three thousand. That night, the Imperial Japanese Navy greeted the soldiers with a frightful display of naval gunnery.

The battleships *Haruna* and *Kongo*, cruising off Lunga Point, blasted Henderson Field with 918 fourteen-inch shells in just two hours, in a bombardment that most of the soldiers would remember as their worst experience on the island. At daylight, the field looked like Swiss cheese, and out of ninety aircraft, only six bombers and five fighters remained operational.

No Swimming

Robert Leckie, a noted military historian and marine veteran of the South Pacific fighting, experienced firsthand the Battle of the Tenaru. In *Helmet for My Pillow*, he describes how the marines cultivated an unlikely ally:

> We never fired at the crocodiles . . . because we considered them a sort of "river patrol." Their appetite for flesh aroused, they seemed to promenade the Tenaru daily. No enemy, we thought, would dare to swim the river with them in it; nor would he succeed if he dared. We relied on our imperfect knowledge of the habits of crocodiles ("If they chase you, run zig-zag, they can't change direction.") and a thick network of barbed wire to forestall their tearing us to pieces. Sometimes on black nights, in a spasm of fear, it might be imagined that the big croc was after us, like the crocodile with the clock inside him who pursues Captain Hook in *Peter Pan*.
>
> So the crocodiles became our darlings, we never molested them. Nor did any of us ever swim the Tenaru again.

Miraculously, only forty-one men had been killed, but hundreds of men were left wandering about in crippling states of shock.

Japanese cruisers continued the offshore bombardment, pouring in another two thousand shells on the Americans in the next two nights. General Vandegrift became concerned that the sustained shelling would fracture his defense. Over the next week, patrol skirmishes were stepped up in the Mataniko River region to the west, and Japanese probes around the American perimeter grew fiercer as

Hyakutake prepared for a decisive assault against the Americans.

The Sendai Offensive, as it became known, finally got under way shortly after dark on 23 October. Hyakutake threw two full infantry regiments of the crack Sendai Division, led by Major General Tadishi Sumiyoshi, against the narrow front defended by the 3rd Battalion, 1st Marines. Artillery and ten eighteen-ton tanks supported Sumiyoshi's attackers. This was a diversion. Meanwhile, the main assault force—some seven thousand Sendai troops under Lieutenant General Masao Maruyama—was snaking its way through a rain-sodden jungle to attack the marine perimeter from the south. Marines of the 1st and 7th Regiments destroyed all of Sumiyoshi's eighteen-tonners with thirty-seven-millimeter anti-tank guns and slaughtered hundreds of enemy infantrymen following behind the tanks. The western assault, which had been launched prematurely, failed.

At noon the next day, General Maruyama issued his final attack order, punctuating it with a personal boast: "I intend to exterminate the enemy around the airfield in one blow."[57] Late that night, in a driving rain, his forces attacked the perimeter east of Bloody Ridge, along a mile-and-a-half front defended by six hundred of Lieutenant Colonel Lewis B. ("Chesty") Puller's 1st Battalion, 7th Marines.

In one sector named Coffin Corner by the marines, the Japanese attacked repeatedly in screaming, grenade-throwing rushes. But with supporting fire from the 2nd Battalion, 164th Infantry, on the left, Puller's men held fast. When Company A ran out of ammunition, Puller directed their company commander to hold with the bayonet.

Throughout a night of wild, shrieking charges, machine-gun section leader Sergeant John Basilone mowed down the attackers by the score. He later explained,

They kept coming, and we kept firing. . . . At dawn our guns were just burned out. Altogether we got rid of 26,000 rounds.[58]

For his cool efficiency and a variety of valorous actions, Basilone was awarded the Medal of Honor, the first marine enlisted man in World War II to earn the nation's highest award. In recommending him for the medal, Colonel Puller wrote that he had "contributed materially to the defeat and virtually the annihilation of a Japanese regiment."[59]

With the issue still in doubt, the 3rd Battalion, 164th Infantry, slogged through the rain and mud to lend a hand to their marine brethren. Their new eight-round M-1 rifles added much-needed firepower to the marines' near-obsolete five-round '03 Springfields. As the superior American firepower began taking its toll, the Japanese charges started tapering off. At dawn, Maruyama called off his attackers. The marines and soldiers had saved the perimeter and Henderson Field. And they had defeated the Japanese in the decisive land

U.S. Army infantrymen help defend Henderson Field during the Sendai Offensive. The soldier in the rear is preparing to fire his magazine-fed M-1 carbine.

the Canal, but the issue of American supremacy was no longer in doubt.

The Initiative Shifts

General Vandegrift spent the next six weeks extending the marine perimeter far enough to prevent Japanese artillery from reaching Henderson Field. With the incremental arrival of the 2nd Marine Division, sent to reinforce and replace weary, casualty-ridden units of the 1st Marine Division, the area under American control was expanded still farther.

On 9 December, Major General Alexander M. Patch, USA, commanding the Army Americal Division, relieved General Vandegrift as commander of Allied operations on Guadalcanal, and the 1st Marine Division was withdrawn.

The Japanese were now on the defensive, entrenched in a heavily defended jungle position about six miles west of Henderson Field and extending inland four miles from Point Cruz. They held this scrap of jungle with fewer than twenty thousand men. By year's end, General Patch opposed them with built-up American forces in the XIV Corps—the Americal, 25th, and 2nd Marine Divisions—totaling about fifty-eight thousand men. Short on supplies and ridden with disease, the Japanese still fought bravely and tenaciously, but the end was already decided.

battle of Guadalcanal. Chesty Puller received his third Navy Cross for his part in the action.

The October campaign cost Hyakutake some thirty-five hundred in dead alone. Maruyama's vaunted Sendai Division was all but wiped out. Combined army and marine casualties totaled fewer than four hundred. In a written commendation for Colonel Bryant Moore of the 164th Infantry, 1st Marines commander Colonel Clifton B. Cates saluted Moore's men for "a most wonderful piece of work," and added, "We are honored to serve with a unit such as yours."[60] There would be more fighting on

The First and the Last

Robert C. Miller, a United Press staff correspondent, landed on Guadalcanal with the first wave of U.S. Marines on 7 August 1942. He covered both the first and last battles on the island. In "Guadalcanal—First Jap Defeat in 1,000 Years" (which appears in *Typewriter Battalion*, edited by Jack Stenbuck), Miller describes the final action:

> GUADALCANAL, Feb. 11, 1943—The battle ended at sundown today in the first complete American victory of the war in the South Pacific, when two American columns working toward the northwestern tip of the island joined forces near Visalie, capturing or annihilating effective Japanese remnants. . . .
>
> Old Glory flies unchallenged over the island.

Her navy smashed repeatedly at sea, her Zeros and Mitsubishis erased from the skies and her proudest regiments now masses of rotting corpses, Japan has tasted defeat for the first time in a thousand years.

To the only correspondent present at the beginning and conclusion of the campaign, it was a magnificent example of American bravery, tenacity and resourcefulness which the enemy was unable at any time to match. . . .

Observers estimated that at least 20,000 Japanese soldiers and marines died in Guadalcanal jungles, many from disease, while another 30,000 died aboard flaming transports and warships blasted by American surface and air units.

After a last, bloody, two-week battle in January 1943, the Japanese withdrew 13,000 of their remaining troops from Guadalcanal in a night evacuation (1–7 February) executed brilliantly by the Imperial Japanese Navy. And so ended one of the longest ground campaigns of the Pacific War. About 50,000 Japanese troops died either on the island or on ships trying to reach there. The Americans lost 1,592 killed and 4,300 wounded—not counting the innumerable victims of the island's vast array of debilitating diseases.

Japanese expansion stopped with the American triumph on Guadalcanal. From 7 August 1942 on, the initiative in the Pacific shifted to the Americans and their allies. But the road to ultimate victory over Japan remained paved with more bloody island battles still to come.

Chapter 4

Tarawa:
Bloody Betio

"The curtain was up in the theatre of death."
—Robert Sherrod, American war correspondent.
"Tarawa: First Day" (in *The War, 1939–1945*,
edited by Desmond Flower and James Reed)

First Lieutenant William Deane Hawkins had a premonition—a glimpse of his own death—when he joined the Marine Corps as a private. Bidding farewell to his best friend, he said prophetically, "I'll see you someday, Mac—but not on this earth."[61] Quick to see action in the South Pacific, he earned a second lieutenant's gold bars on Tulagi, at the start of the Guadalcanal campaign.

At 0855 on Saturday, 20 November 1943, the twenty-nine-year-old commander of the Scout-Sniper Platoon of the 2nd Marine Regiment led five men into Betio islet—fifteen minutes in advance of the first assault wave at Tarawa Atoll. The six men clambered up a seaplane ramp at the tip of the 550-yard-long pier. The pier jutted out into the lagoon from the north side

of the coral islet. Hawkins and his men raced along it. The rest of his platoon of thirty-four expert fighters trailed in two landing craft; a third carried Second Lieutenant Alan G. Leslie Jr. and his flame-throwing engineers. Hawkins signaled them to join him. Their mission: to neutralize the pier.

The Japanese had built the long pier to house latrines over the water. It split the designated landing beaches and was currently infested with riflemen and machine gunners who could bring raking fire to bear on the marine LVTs (landing vehicle, tracked) headed their way. Suddenly, the Japanese opened fire on Hawkins and his men, igniting gasoline drums stored on the wharf. Hawkins waved most of his men back and began fighting down the length of the pier

49

with four scouts and Leslie, who burned out two latrines filled with machine gunners with his flamethrower. They fought yard by yard and hand to hand, with rifle butt and bayonet. But with the midsection of the pier engulfed in roaring flames, Hawkins and his men could clear only half of it. The inshore end of the pier remained infested with Japanese gunners, who brought hellacious fire to bear on the oncoming marines for the rest of D day at Tarawa.

Operation Galvanic

Admiral Chester W. Nimitz's long-awaited offensive in the Central Pacific Area finally got under way in November 1943. Battle planners, who like to assign code names to their brain trusts, called it Operation Galvanic. The plan called for the simultaneous seizures of Tarawa and Makin Atolls in the Gilbert Islands. Since his victory at Midway, Nimitz had spent his time studying new concepts in naval warfare, while American shipyards were rebuilding—and adding to—his fleet. Now, with the devastation of the Pearl Harbor attack long since repaired and his anchorage bulging with new, faster, more highly specialized warships, he felt ready to make his move.

To lead his forces westward along the sea routes to Japan, Nimitz handpicked the three very best commanders the sea services had to offer: Vice Admiral Raymond A. Spruance to command the Central Pacific Force (later the 5th Fleet); Rear Admiral Richmond K. Turner to head up Spruance's amphibious forces (responsible

for transporting troops and supplies from ship to shore); and Major General Holland M. ("Howlin' Mad") Smith to command V Amphibious Corps (the tens of thousands of soldiers and marines who would spearhead the greatest sustained amphibious campaign ever conceived).

Operation Galvanic commenced on 11 November 1943, when Admiral Turner's invasion fleet shaped course for the Gilbert Islands chain. Turner's forces were divided into two groups. Task Force (TF) 53, the northern attack group, was made up of the LSTs (landing ship, tank) and transports carrying some sixty-five hundred soldiers of the 27th Infantry Division, four battleships, four heavy cruisers, four escort carriers, and thirteen destroyers. Admiral Turner took personal command of TF 53, assigned to assault Makin Atoll, about one hundred miles to the north of Tarawa. The southern attack force, TF 52, comprised sixteen transports carrying eighteen thousand troops of the 2nd Marine Division, and was accompanied by a powerful bombardment force of three battleships, three heavy cruisers, five escort carriers, and twenty-one destroyers. Turner, electing to accompany TF 53 because of Makin's closer proximity to the Japanese Combined Fleet and its potential intervention, assigned command of TF 52 to his deputy Rear Admiral Harry W. Hill.

Admiral Hill's task force departed its staging base at Efate, in the New Hebrides, on 11 November 1943. Its destination was an island code-named Helen. Hill did not

Vice Admiral Raymond A. Spruance (left), Rear Admiral Richmond K. Turner (center, with binoculars), and Major General Holland M. ("Howlin' Mad") Smith (right).

disclose their objective until the convoy had been at sea for seventy-two hours, when he announced:

> Just six days from today at 0830 we're going to hit Tarawa Atoll in the Gilbert Islands. We're going to land on this island at the end of the atoll; the natives call it Betio. Before we land on the place, we're going to pound it with naval shell fire and dive bombers. We're going to steamroller that place until hell wouldn't have it.[62]

Lookouts aboard the battleship *Maryland*—one of the sunken battlewagons raised and refitted from the depths of Pearl Harbor—sighted Betio's outline on the horizon by the light of a quarter moon at 0200 on 20 November. Marines of the 2nd Division had begun lining up for special breakfasts of steak and eggs two hours earlier—this would be the last breakfast for more than a thousand of them.

By 0430, the first wave of marines was in the water, churning toward the line of departure in LVTs or circling about in LCVPs (landing craft, vehicle, personnel) waiting to form up behind the tracked vehicles. (The line of departure is the line from which landing craft begin their run to the beach.) Ten minutes later, Japanese batteries on Betio's south shore opened fire on the invasion fleet with a pair of eight-inch coastal guns captured at Singapore. American naval guns—sixteen-inch on down to five-inch—responded with a thunderous offshore barrage, silencing the onshore guns and continuing for two and a half hours. They poured three thousand tons of high explosives into the islet, pausing twice for early- and late-arriving air strikes by U.S. carrier planes.

"Surely, we all thought, no mortal man could live through such destroying power,"[63] said *Time* correspondent Robert Sherrod. But they were all *wrong*, as the utility-clad shock troops of Major General Julian C. Smith's 2nd Marine Division were about to learn in the coral and blood that was Betio. The war planners in Washington called it Operation Galvanic; the marines at Tarawa called it Hell.

Day One: Morning

Tarawa Atoll—the prime target of Operation Galvanic—lies about ninety miles north of the equator. It comprises a chain of islets in a triangular reef around a lagoon about eighteen miles long by some thirteen miles wide. Betio, an islet three miles long by six hundred yards wide at its widest point, lies in the southwest corner of the atoll. The Americans wanted it for their airfield, from which they hoped to advance up the island chain into the Marshall Islands (Kwajalein and Eniwetok).

The Japanese garrison on Betio, commanded by Rear Admiral Keiji Shibasaki, consisted of the 7th Special Landing Force—called *rikusentai*—and the 3rd

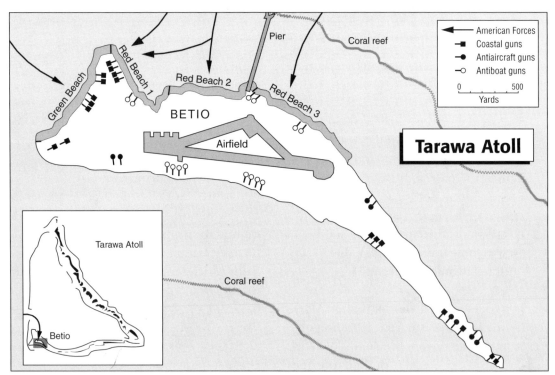

Special Base Force, plus attached naval personnel and a technically noncombatant labor force. The *rikusentai* were elite troops, the Japanese equivalent of U.S. Marines. Altogether, Shibasaki's forces totaled 4,836—2,619 fighting troops and 2,217 other personnel.

Betio's defenders were solidly ensconced in low, flat pillboxes, constructed of six layers of coconut logs and reinforced by sand, concrete, and steel. They proved almost impervious to the offshore shelling and aerial attacks. The islet also bristled with gun emplacements, generously affixed with deadly dual-purpose antiair/antiboat guns, ranging from 75 millimeters to 127 millimeters.

Admiral Shibasaki, exuding confidence in his *rikusentai* and five hundred pillboxes and gun emplacements, often boasted, "A million men cannot take Tarawa in a hundred years."[64] Bravado aside, however, his mission on Tarawa was to hold the atoll for at least seventy-two hours—the time it would take the Japanese Combined Fleet to steam thirteen hundred miles from Truk Lagoon and engage the U.S. Pacific Fleet in a decisive sea battle. Unknown to Shibasaki, however, help from the Combined Fleet would not be forthcoming, because it had lost many of its aircraft in operations against American landings on Bougainville.

Shibasaki anticipated a landing on Betio's south shore and concentrated his defenses there. But the Americans elected to attack from the lagoon side of the islet, where the marines could land on broad beaches. Looking south, the beaches were designated Red Beach 2, to the right of the base of the pier, the central beach; Red Beach 1 to its right; and Red Beach 3 to its left, on the other side of the pier. A fourth beach to the right of Red Beach 1, at the western end of the islet, was designated Green Beach. Attacking from the lagoon side entailed the danger of dealing with unpredictable neap tides—called "dodging tides" by the natives—that often remained in or out for a whole day. At low tide, the LCVPs would bottom out on the coral reef that formed the lagoon on the westward side. Admiral Turner gambled that the tides would run in his favor. He lost.

In advance of the landing parties, two minesweepers knifed through a narrow break in the reef and entered the lagoon to clear it of mines. Two destroyers followed and raked Betio's north shore with their five-inchers. With the first waves of LVTs (called amtracs or amphtracs) wallowing shoreward, Admiral Hill lifted his offshore bombardment at 0855, estimating that the LVTs were within five minutes of the beach. The LVTs were actually fifteen minutes away, but concussion from the admiral's sixteen-inch guns had knocked out his principal radio network and many of the landing force networks. Communications became an instant disaster. Hill also could not see the LVTs through the veil of smoke and morning mist that blanketed the islet. Fearing that he might hit his marines, Hill refused to resume firing. Shibasaki used those few minutes to shift most of his troops from the south shore to the lagoon side of Betio.

The tide was out when the first three waves of LVTs hit the westward reef. They clambered over it, and despite the murderous fire from the beaches, all but eight of the eighty-seven attack vehicles landed safely. In ten minutes, Colonel David M. Shoup, onshore assault commander and commander of the 2nd Marines, had fifteen hundred marines ashore, hugging the coconut-log seawall along Betio's north shore. Then disaster struck.

The marines had hoped there would be a high tide by midmorning to float the LCVPs (often called "Higgins boats" after their inventor) over the reefs. They did not get one. The LCVPs of the fourth and fifth

---

Under heavy fire, LVTs crawl over a reef at Betio's north shore. Unlike Higgins boats, these tracked vehicles could land troops at low tide.

waves ran aground on the partially exposed reefs or milled about helplessly outside them, some five hundred to six hundred yards from shore. A withering crossfire from the shore and from the hulk of a sunken Japanese ship northwest of the pier played havoc with the hapless Higgins boats.

No less than 20 of them "full of dead and wounded were stuck on the reef," wrote Samuel Eliot Morison. "One large gun [ashore] was horribly accurate; several times it dropped a shell right on a landing craft just as the ramp came down, spreading a pool of blood around the boat."[65] Only the 38 remaining LVTs (125 in all) made it over the coral barrier.

Empty LVTs from the first waves ferried some of the stranded marines ashore, but most of them had to struggle through several hundred yards of shoulder-high water, lashed by machine-gun bullets. "We had seven hundred yards to walk slowly into that machine gun [sic] fire, looming into large targets as we rose onto higher ground," reported Robert Sherrod, who landed with the fourth wave. "I was scared as I had never been scared before."[66]

Later, Colonel Shoup, who also came in with the fourth wave, and was wounded in the leg, told Sherrod, "This is the damnedest crap game I have ever got into."[67] Shoup, directing the battle while standing waist-deep in water, was still unable to make it all the way to shore.

Division commander Julian Smith ordered a battalion of the 8th Marines—his reserve regiment—ashore. Thirty percent of their first wave reached the beach; less of the second wave arrived. The third wave was all but obliterated. At a little after 1130, Julian Smith, still without radio contact with the landing force, but sensing that his division was fighting for its life, radioed Admiral Turner off Makin:

> Request release of Combat Team 6 [three battalions of the 6th Marines, the corps reserve, already present in transports off Betio]. Issue in doubt.[68]

"Issue in doubt." Marines of the first wave take cover on Betio as one marine treats a wounded comrade.

Smith's message intentionally echoed the last words received from the doomed marines on Wake Island. Less than an hour later Smith received an affirmative answer. He now had four uncommitted battalions—the 1st Battalion, 8th Marines, and three battalions of the 6th Marines. Smith ordered 1/8 ashore, but they did not receive his message and spent the night afloat in Higgins boats.

Meanwhile, Colonel Shoup finally reached the beach on his hands and knees at noon. He and a few of his staff quickly set up a command post on Red Beach 2 at the base of a huge pillbox, still occupied by several scores of Japanese. By nightfall, of the five thousand marines who had landed, fifteen hundred were dead or wounded, and the remainder were clinging precariously to two narrow beachheads, neither more than three hundred yards deep.

No one needed to tell Colonel Shoup that the issue was *indeed* in doubt.

STRATEGIC BATTLES IN THE PACIFIC

Day Two

Had Admiral Shibasaki chosen to counter-attack that first night, his forces might well have driven the marines back into the sea. But no attack came. Unknown to the marines for the next fifty years, Shibasaki had been killed that first day by a shell burst when caught outside his pillbox. The loss of their leader, their communications, and half of their troops to the heavy American bombardment negated any enemy capability for launching a coordinated counterattack.

During the night, Japanese fire slacked off enough to enable American landing craft to approach the end of the pier and unload the first artillery pieces and urgently needed medical supplies and plasma for the wounded awaiting evacuation onshore. But at dawn, disaster struck again.

When the 1st Battalion, 8th Marines, finally approached the beach after spending all night in their boats, Japanese snipers in the wrecked hulk and on the shore gave them a hot welcome. The tide was low again, the boats ran aground on the reefs again, and the marines were forced to wade ashore for hundreds of yards again. Their losses were heavier than on the first day.

As if crazed by the sight of such slaughter, Lieutenant Deane Hawkins ran amok among the pillboxes still dominating Red Beach 2. Armed only with a few grenades and superhuman courage, he single-handedly attacked bunker after bunker, stuffing grenades into any available opening—firing slits, vent tubes, back entrances—until struck down by a 7.7-millimeter Nambu machine-gun round. He died in ten minutes. With his broken-hearted scout-snipers gathered around him, he said at the last, "Boys, I sure hate to leave you like this."[69] The marines named Betio's airfield "Hawkins Field" in his honor and later presented a Medal of Honor to his family. His citation read:

> His relentless fighting spirit in the face of formidable opposition and his exceptionally daring tactics served as an inspiration to his comrades during the most crucial phase of the battle.[70]

Hawkins had fulfilled his premonition of death. Colonel Shoup later credited him with winning the battle for Tarawa.

The colonel himself would later receive the Medal of Honor for his dauntless, rock-steady direction of the fierce fighting. Shoup was the only marine to earn the Medal of Honor on Betio and live to wear it. He later became the twenty-second commandant of the Marine Corps.

At noon the capricious neap tide rose at last. Four destroyers cruised the shoreline, pummeling enemy pillboxes and gun emplacements with their five-inch guns. The Higgins boats could now scrape over the reefs, and marines stormed ashore throughout the afternoon. With the aid of additional artillery and tanks, Shoup's forces advanced across Betio's narrow waist and split the Japanese defense in two. By late afternoon, the 1st Battalion, 6th Marines, along with a platoon of light tanks, had landed almost without a scratch. With his tanks now driving against enemy pillboxes and strong points on either flank, he radioed General Smith (the radio net was now operational): "Casualties many. Dead unknown. Combat efficiency—we are winning!"[71]

That night, Colonel Merritt A. Edson, now Julian Smith's chief of staff, came ashore to assume overall command on Tarawa. And marine artillery units set up on nearby Bairiki Island to help bombard Japanese positions on Betio. While Colonel Edson mapped out his strategy for the coming day, the Japanese radio on Betio transmitted its last message: "Our weapons have been destroyed and from now on everyone is attempting a final charge. . . . May Japan exist for ten thousand years."[72]

Day Three

During the third day, which bore scant resemblance to the first day and a half, the marines seized control of the situation. The 1st Battalion, 6th Marines, driving eastward from Green Beach, advanced some eight hundred yards down the length of the airfield before noon. Colonel Shoup led his 2nd Marines westward in a violent attack against the Pocket, a six-hundred-yard gap separating his forces on Red Beach 2 from a small group isolated on Red Beach 1. By dark, the marines occupied the western two-thirds of the islet. Julian Smith, who had come ashore earlier, took personal command of his division.

Clearing a Pillbox

Robert Sherrod, a *Time* correspondent, landed with the fourth wave of marines at Tarawa. In the following extract from Ronald H. Spector's *Eagle Against the Sun*, Sherrod describes how marines typically cleared pillboxes on Betio:

A Marine jumped over the seawall and began throwing blocks of TNT into a coconut-log pillbox. . . . Two more Marines scaled the seawall, one of them carrying a twin-cylindered tank strapped to his shoulders, the other holding the nozzle of a flame thrower. As another charge of TNT boomed inside the pillbox, causing smoke and dust to billow out, a khaki-clad figure ran out the side entrance. The flame thrower, waiting for him, caught him in its withering stream of intense fire. As soon as it touched him, the Jap flared up like a piece of celluloid. He was dead instantly but the bullets in his cartridge belt exploded for a full sixty seconds after he had been charred to nothingness.

A Japanese pillbox made of steel plate stands gutted after having been cleared by marines.

The promised "final charge" came that night.

The remaining *rikusentai* launched a series of banzai attacks against the 1st Battalion, 6th Marines. Stupefied with sake and armed with rifles, swords, bayonets, knives, and grenades, they struck in waves, hurling themselves at the marines again and again. Marine artillery and naval gunfire killed many of them instantly; marine machine-gun and small-arms fire stopped many more. But some broke through the marine perimeter, and the battle turned into one-on-one, hand-to-hand savagery, prosecuted with bayonet, knife, and swinging rifles. The marines proved their case. When the sun shone again on the tiny islet, the marines counted the mangled bodies of 325 dead Japanese around their perimeter. Two days of mopping up remained to be done, but for all practical purposes the battle for bloody Betio was over.

The Pacific Timetable

At 1330 that afternoon, General Julian Smith announced the end of organized resistance on Tarawa. After seventy-six hours of fighting, in a space not as big as New York City's Central Park, marine casualties numbered 3,407, with 1 out of every 3 killed—a greater toll than Guadalcanal had exacted in six months of tough fighting. Of 4,836 Japanese

at Tarawa, only 146 survived—17 *rikusentai* and 129 Korean laborers.

A hundred miles to the north, at 1030 the previous morning, General Ralph C. Smith, commander of the army's 27th Division forces, had already signaled "MAKIN TAKEN."[73] His losses, much smaller than at Tarawa due to substantially lighter resistance, totaled 64 killed and 150 wounded. So ended Operation Galvanic.

Newspaper photographs of marine corpses floating on the tide or piled up in front of coconut abutments stunned an American public previously conditioned to viewing the war through the lens of government censorship and exaggerated reports of Allied successes. Later, after the release of the uncensored documentary film *With the Marines at Tarawa*, shot on the scene by marine combat photographers, Robert Sherrod asked Brigadier General Robert Denig, Marine Corps public rela-

Photographs of dead marines at Tarawa shocked Americans at home. The public had previously been shielded from seeing the true cost of Allied successes.

The High Cost of Sand and Coral

The U.S. Marines captured the sandy, coral islets of Tarawa Atoll at a dreadful cost of human life. Where courage was a common commodity, the valorous deeds of three men merited their nation's highest award posthumously.

First Lieutenant William Deane Hawkins, who sensed the nearness of his own death when he joined the marines, lived long enough to become a Marine Corps legend. He crawled forward into withering fire from five enemy machine guns to destroy a pillbox. Although seriously wounded in the chest, he refused to be evacuated and destroyed three more pillboxes before being wounded again, this time mortally.

Another first lieutenant, Alexander "Sandy" Bonneyman, led a charge of flamethrower operators and demolition men up the slopes of a huge Japanese bunker and dropped thermite grenades down their air vents. When hundreds of the enemy poured out the rear of the bunker, the 8th Marines rose into action and fired at them. But Bonneyman, kneeling on top of the bunker and shouting for more explosives, fell over dead from a Japanese sniper bullet.

Staff Sergeant William J. Bordelon, a combat engineer, inspired his men with a superlative display of courage and aggressiveness. He personally assaulted and destroyed three pillboxes with explosive satchel charges. Although wounded, he seized a fresh charge and attacked a fourth pillbox, but his luck ran out and the enemy shot him dead.

All three of these extraordinary men earned the Medal of Honor on Betio; all three of these exemplary marines paid the high cost of sand and coral.

tions chief, what sort of effect it had on the corps itself. "A strong one," Denig answered. "Enlistments are down thirty-five percent."[74]

The Americans learned a number of lessons at Tarawa and applied them in future operations. Tests conducted later against specially constructed pillboxes revealed that high-angle (lobbing) fire was far more effective against them than straight-trajectory fire. Tracked vehicles had proved their value. More were ordered, with better armaments and thicker armor designed into them. A need for improvements in communications, hydrographic intelligence, close air support, and assault weapons was also recognized and acted on. And new, specially fitted command ships were developed for task-force amphibious commanders to replace ill-suited battleships and cruisers. The marines paid for every lesson learned at Tarawa with their blood.

Even today, military experts still argue about whether the lessons learned were worth their cost. It is likely that the arguments will never be settled. One thing is certain: The greatest number of casualties at Betio resulted from the shallow water over the reef, which forced so many marines to wade hundreds of yards to shore. The wholesale slaughter of countless marines might have been avoided had the operation been delayed until a full moon guaranteed a high tide. But that would have meant upsetting the Pacific timetable.

Chapter 5

Leyte Gulf: The Greatest Naval Battle

"I didn't think we'd last fifteen minutes, but I thought we might as well give them all we've got before we went down."
— Rear Admiral Clifton A. F. Sprague, commander of Task Unit 77.4.3 (quoted in Nathan Miller, *The Naval Air War*)

Two and a half years after the fall of Corregidor, and less than a year after the Tarawa campaign, the twin island-hopping campaigns of General Douglas MacArthur and Admiral Chester W. Nimitz converged in the Philippines. The general, fulfilling his promise to return to the islands that he had been ordered to leave many long months before, landed on Leyte with the U.S. 6th Army on 20 October 1944. In defense of MacArthur's return and the start of Allied efforts to reclaim the Philippines, the U.S. Navy confronted the Imperial Japanese Navy in the greatest naval battle in history.

Return to the Philippines

By October 1944, the mostly American forces under MacArthur and Nimitz had advanced in tandem in the Western Pacific and now occupied Morotai, Saipan, Guam, Tinian, and Peleliu-Angaur. The Americans now stood poised only three hundred miles from the southernmost Philippine island of Mindanao. A month earlier, in a meeting in Quebec on 12 September, President Roosevelt and Prime Minister Winston Churchill had drafted plans for the occupation of Germany and the defeat of Japan. They set 20 October 1944 as the date for the U.S. invasion of the Philippines under MacArthur.

On 14 October, an enormous U.S. amphibious armada of more than 700 vessels set course from New Guinea ports for the coast of Leyte. Aboard the vessels of Admiral Thomas C. Kinkaid's U.S. 7th Fleet, some 200,000 troops of General Walter

Krueger's U.S. 6th Army were en route to their destination in the central Philippines. Kinkaid's vast flotilla included 157 combatant ships; 420 amphibious vessels; 84 patrol, minesweeping, and hydrographic craft (for charting the waters and measuring depth and flow); and 73 service ships.

For the actual assault on Leyte, the 7th Fleet would be split into three groups, two assigned to landing operations and a third to direct support. The Northern Attack Force, designated Task Force (TF) 78, comprised Vice Admiral Daniel E. Barbey's 7th Amphibious Force, which had operated with MacArthur throughout the Southwest Pacific campaigns. The Southern Attack

Force, Task Force 79, consisted of Vice Admiral Thomas S. Wilkinson's 3rd Amphibious Force, which had been transferred to the 7th Fleet from Admiral William F. Halsey's 3rd Fleet. This freed Halsey—reputed to be "profane, aggressive, rash, impulsive, likable, an indifferent administrator, and sincere"[75]—to use his fleet as a mobile

During the Leyte campaign, Admiral William F. Halsey (right) planned to use the 3rd Fleet (below) as a mobile striking force against the Japanese Combined Fleet.

striking force and concentrate on the Japanese Combined Fleet, as necessary. Task Force 77, assigned to the direct support functions, was made up of the 7th Fleet's battleships (BBs), heavy and light cruisers (CAs and CLs), destroyers (DDs), and escort carriers (CVEs).

Seventh Fleet commander Kinkaid, once described as "a black-eyed, rosy-cheeked, noisy Irishman who loves a rough-house,"[76] retained overall command of TF 77. He further subdivided it into several specialized task groups, the most notable of which were Task Groups 77.2 and 77.4. They would soon provide their rosy-cheeked fleet commander with enough roughhousing to last a lifetime.

Under Admiral Kinkaid, Rear Admiral Jesse B. Oldendorf commanded Task Group 77.2, the Fire and Bombardment Group. It contained six old battleships, five cruisers, and fifteen destroyers. Task Group 77.4, under Rear Admiral Thomas L. Sprague, consisted of eighteen escort carriers and their escorting destroyers, divided among units Taffy 1 through 3 (TG 4.2.1–3). It was responsible for coordinated air strikes.

The 3rd Fleet under Halsey contributed a massive air punch to the already considerable striking power of the 7th Fleet. Without its detached amphibious force, the 3rd Fleet consisted primarily of Task Force 38, a carrier striking force commanded by Vice Admiral Marc A. Mitscher. TF 38 was split into four groups (TG 38.1–4). Each group typically contained two fleet carriers (CVs) and two light carriers (CVLs), which were supported in varying proportions by six battleships, fifteen cruisers, and forty-eight destroyers.

This vast array of American military power bearing down on the Philippines seemed to bode well for a favorable outcome to the impending invasion and MacArthur's successful return. But there are no guarantees in warfare, and this operation almost failed because of one potentially fatal flaw: a split command. Admiral Kinkaid reported to General MacArthur; Admiral Halsey answered to Admiral Nimitz. The absence of a single command would later prove troublesome as the great sea battle unfolded in Philippine waters.

Operation Victory One

Meanwhile, having anticipated an American move against the Philippines, the Japanese Imperial General Headquarters had prepared a defense strategy for the vital archipelago. They could ill afford to lose the Philippines, the loss of which would cut their vital supply line to essential raw materials in the Southwest Pacific. They called their plan Operation Victory One (*Sho Ichi Go* in Japanese). Their strategists also drew up three alternate defense plans to deal with potential American strikes elsewhere—from Formosa to the northernmost Japanese home island of Hokkaido. According to naval historian Samuel Eliot Morison, however, Japanese intelligence was "betting on the Philippines."[77] They won their bet.

On the morning of 17 October, the Japanese 16th Army Command alerted Tokyo of an enemy force approaching Leyte. Japanese army and navy commands flashed coded radio messages to execute *Sho Ichi Go*, or *Sho*-1, that afternoon.

The Northern Force, under Vice Admiral Jisaburo Ozawa, consisted of Japan's 4 remaining carriers, 2 battleships, 3 cruisers, and 8 destroyers. It set sail from Japan toward Luzon to lure Halsey's 3rd Fleet northward—away from the landing area—to attack Ozawa's carriers. Ozawa's carriers were virtually powerless, having already lost all but 116 of their aircraft earlier in the month to raids on Formosa and Okinawa by Halsey's aircraft and others. Also, Ozawa's pilots were only half-trained and certainly no match for the veteran American fliers. But Halsey, of course, would have no way of knowing that Ozawa's lure was a hollow ruse.

Vice Admiral Takeo Kurita's Center Force (or First Attack Force)—the main force—steamed northeastward from Malaya, Borneo, and the China Sea to traverse the San Bernardino Strait. His fleet comprised two superbattleships, three other battleships, twelve cruisers, and fifteen destroyers.

The Southern Force (or C Force) of Vice Admiral Shoji Nishimura consisted of two battleships, one heavy cruiser, and four destroyers proceeding east from Malaya and Borneo. It was reinforced by Vice Admiral Kiyohide Shima's Second Attack Force of two heavy and one light cruisers and four destroyers out of the Ryukyu Islands. According to the plan, Shima was to steam southeast and rendezvous with Nishimura's western forces at the Surigao Strait between Mindanao and Leyte. Kurita's Center

Operation Victory One

OZAWA

LUZON

TASK FORCE 38 (Halsey's Third Fleet)

Manila

Bataan Peninsula

Corregidor

San Bernardino Strait

KURITA

Palawan Passage

Sibuyan Sea

SAMAR

Leyte Gulf

Mindanao Sea

Surigao Strait

NISHIMURA

MINDANAO

BORNEO

U.S.
Japanese

Force and Nishimura's Southern Force would then form pincers to crush Admiral Kinkaid's 7th Fleet and destroy his landing forces at Leyte, marooning American troops ashore.

In its purest sense, the naval role in the "Victory One" plan was a last-ditch gamble by the Combined Fleet to lure the American fleet into the so-called great decisive sea battle long sought by the Imperial Japanese Navy (IJN). Its success relied on the closely coordinated efforts of three naval elements, on the IJN's superior night-fighting ability, and on the rash aggressiveness of Admiral Halsey.

The *Sho*-1 plan almost succeeded, not as one "decisive" battle but as separate sea actions in the Sibuyan Sea and Surigao Strait and off Samar and Cape Engaño.

Battle of the Sibuyan Sea

On the morning of 20 October 1944, General Krueger's U.S. 6th Army began landing on Leyte. That afternoon General Douglas MacArthur came ashore, announced his return to the people of the Philippines, and implored them, in part, to

Rally to me! Let the indomitable spirit of Bataan and Corregidor lead on. As the lines of battle roll forward to bring you within the zone of operations, rise and strike. . . . Let no heart be faint. Let every arm be steeled.[78]

By midnight, 132,000 American troops and 200,000 tons of equipment and supplies had landed on Leyte to begin the land battle for the island.

On 22 October, the Japanese Northern Force left Japan while the Center and Southern Forces were converging on the central Philippines. Admiral Kurita's Center Force entered the Palawan Passage from the South China Sea early the next morning. Two American submarines, *Darter* and *Dace,* were patrolling together at cruising speed on the surface of the reef-studded passage when blips started appearing on their radar screens, signaling that there was an indeterminate number of ships at a range of fifteen miles. Commander David H. McClintock, *Darter's* skipper, raised his megaphone and shouted over to *Dace:* "Let's go!" The submarines poured the oil to their diesels and gave chase. They soon made out a large formation of capital ships, flanked by a screen of destroyers. *Darter* alerted Admiral Halsey of an enemy in sight, then closed in on the Japanese formation. In Commander McClintock's words,

At 0525 the first target could be identified as a heavy cruiser with huge bow waves. . . . At 0527 all tubes were ready . . . range under 3,000 yards. . . . Now the angle on the bow was getting bigger . . . range under a thousand . . . shooting bearing . . . mark . . . fire one! [Then five more!] Shift targets to the second cruiser . . . bearing mark . . . fire seven! The first stern torpedo is on its way.[79]

The first cruiser, Kurita's flagship *Atago*, sank with 359 men aboard. A destroyer picked up Kurita and his staff. McClintock's stern torpedoes badly damaged *Takeo*, the second cruiser. Meanwhile, the cruiser *Maya*, struck by three of *Dace*'s torpedoes, blew up and sank four minutes later.

Kurita transferred his flag to the battleship *Yamato* and, after calming a momentary panic that had swept over his fleet, pressed on toward Leyte. Admiral Halsey immediately ordered a massive air strike on the Center Force for the next day, designating three of Admiral Mitscher's four task groups for the action. But the Japanese struck first.

On 24 October, seventy-six planes from Ozawa's Northern Force struck Halsey's 3rd Fleet. They scored their first success when a lone Judy dive-bomber slipped through an umbrella of American Hellcats and dropped two 550-pound bombs directly into the torpedo storage area of the CVL *Princeton*. The light carrier erupted in a huge explosion, spewing flaming debris down on the cruiser *Birmingham*. One of its officers later declared:

The spectacle that greeted the human eye was terrible to behold. Dead, dying, and wounded, many of them badly and horribly, covered the decks. . . . Blood ran freely down our waterways, and continued to run for some time.[80]

After the initial assault on Leyte, American troops prepare to unload equipment and supplies from two LSTs (landing ship, tank).

The *Birmingham*, although only slightly damaged, took losses of 229 dead and 420 wounded; the *Princeton*, beyond salvage, was abandoned and torpedoed. The Japanese lost 56 aircraft.

Halsey struck back with a fury that same day, sending some 259 planes from TG 38.2 and TG 38.3 across Leyte to attack Kurita's Center Force in the Sibuyan Sea. The American pilots worked over his fleet in five separate attacks, with the *Musashi* bearing the brunt of their efforts. After absorbing 19 torpedo and 17 bomb hits, the superbattleship finally plunged to the bottom, stern first, with half of its 2,400-man complement. Its sister ship *Yamato*, the smaller battleships *Nagato* and *Haruna,* and the light cruiser *Yahagi* suffered some damage; the heavy cruiser *Myoko* had to return to Brunei for repairs. Kurita then retired his fleet westward but doubled back after dark and continued on toward his rendezvous at Leyte.

The next day, 25 October, Halsey—believing Kurita to be on the run—finally took Ozawa's bait and struck out after the Japanese carriers. His decision to turn northward left the Leyte beachhead uncovered. History's greatest sea fight then fragmented into three separate engagements.

The guns of Admiral Oldendorf's TG 77.2 open fire on Admiral Nishimura's fleet in Surigao Strait. The Japanese battleships Yamashiro *and* Fuso *were sunk in the night engagement.*

Battle of Surigao Strait

Just before midnight on 24–25 October, on a dark, moonless night, Admiral Nishimura's Southern Force approached the western end of the Surigao Strait between Leyte, Dinagat, and Mindanao Islands. His four destroyers led the way, in line, followed by the two battleships *Yamashiro* and *Fuso* and, bringing up the rear of the column, the heavy cruiser *Mogami*. Admiral Shima's Second Attack Force trailed twenty miles behind.

Suddenly, a flotilla of PT boats—thirty-nine in all—appeared out of the darkness and attacked the column in successive waves. The speedy boats launched all of their torpedoes and raced off into the shadows without scoring a hit. But they radioed the course, speed, and formation of

Nishimura's column to the U.S. 7th Fleet, whereupon Admiral Kinkaid prepared a proper welcome for the enemy vessels. "Prepare for a night engagement,"[81] he ordered Admiral Oldendorf.

Oldendorf positioned TG 77.2's six battleships and eight cruisers in a double line of battle blocking the sixteen-mile exit to the strait and deployed twenty-eight destroyers in the narrow waters ahead of them. Aboard the destroyer *Remey*, flagship of Destroyer Squadron 54 (Desron 54), Commander R. P. Fiala addressed his crew over the loudspeaker just before 0300:

> This is the Captain speaking. Tonight our ship has been designated to make the first torpedo run on the Jap task force that is on its way to stop our landings in Leyte Gulf. It is our job to stop the Japs.[82]

And stop them they did. The destroyers attacked the enemy column on both flanks, launching their first torpedoes at 0301. In less than half an hour, the fast little fighting ships of Desron 54 crippled Nishimura's fleet, damaging his flagship *Yamashiro*, setting the *Fuso* aflame, sinking the destroyer *Yamagumo*, and knocking two other destroyers out of the action. Admiral Nishimura ordered his warships to "proceed and attack all ships."[83] It was his last command. The *Yamashiro* led the way, followed by the *Mogami* and *Shigure*.

Admiral Oldendorf, aboard the cruiser *Louisville*, his flagship, awaited their arrival.

At 0400, he gave the order to open fire. He later recalled,

> It seemed as if every ship in the flank forces and the battle line opened up at once, and there was a semi-circle of fire which landed squarely on one point, which was the leading battleship. The semi-circle of fire so confused the Japanese that they did not know what target to shoot at. I remember seeing one or two salvos start toward my flagship but in the excitement of the occasion I forgot to look where they landed.[84]

In the twenty minutes after Oldendorf's order to fire, the guns of TF 77 fired off more than 3,250 shells. Nishimura's flagship *Yamashiro* took numerous hits in its superstructure, then another American torpedo in its powder magazine. At 0419, the battleship rolled over and sank with Nishimura's flag still flying. Most of its twelve-hundred-man crew went with it. The burning *Fuso*, trailing several miles astern, finally succumbed to its flames and joined its sister ship a few minutes later. The *Mogami* and *Shigure* turned and fled.

The swift *Shigure* escaped, making thirty-five knots. But when *Mogami* hauled about amid the pandemonium, it rammed and severely damaged Admiral Shima's flagship *Nachi*. Shima took that as a bad omen, apparently, for he turned his ships around and headed for the open sea. American planes caught up with both crippled ships four hours later and sank them.

Double Damage

In the Battle of the Sibuyan Sea, the Americans lost one PT boat; and the U.S. destroyer *Albert W. Grant*, mistaken for a Japanese warship, was severely damaged by friendly fire. To make matters worse, Japanese guns also opened up on the hapless *Grant*. Thomas J. Cutler's *The Battle of Leyte Gulf* contains the following entry from the destroyer's log:

0408 1/2 Additional shell hits began to riddle ship. Hit forward at water line flooded forward storeroom and forward crew's berthing compartment. Hit in 40mm gun #1 exploded 40mm ammunition and started fire. Hit through starboard boat davit exploded killing ship's doctor, Lieutenant Charles Akin Mathier, five radiomen, and almost entire amidships repair party. Other hits in forward stack, one hit on port motor whaleboat, one hit and low order explosion in galley. One hit in scullery room, one hit in after crew's berthing compartment, and one hit in forward engine room. All lights, telephone communications, radars, and radios out of commission. Steering control shifted aft.

Cutler comments, "It is difficult to imagine what was *not* hit on that ship."

The Battle of the Surigao Strait cost the Japanese two thirty-six-thousand-ton battleships, two heavy cruisers, and three destroyers, a heavy price to pay for totally failing in their mission. Conversely, the Americans lost one PT boat and damaged one of their own destroyers with friendly fire.

Action off Cape Engaño

At dawn, on 25 October, following the 7th Fleet's resounding victory in the Sibuyan Sea, Admiral Halsey's 3rd Fleet caught up with Admiral Ozawa's Northern Force off Cape Engaño of northeastern Luzon. Vice Admiral Marc A. Mitscher sent the pilots and planes of Task Force 38 after them. At 0800, his Helldivers (dive-bombers) plunged down on the Japanese carriers. Then a flight of Avengers (torpedo-bombers) swept in off the wave tops. For the next ten hours, six successive air strikes pummeled Ozawa's near-defenseless carriers and their escorts with bombs and torpedoes.

The elated American pilots took few casualties and could scarcely contain their excitement. One young pilot, upon his return to the *Lexington*, clambered up the ladder to Mitscher's command post in the carrier's island and shouted at the sober-faced admiral, "I got a hit on a carrier! I got a hit on a carrier!"[85] And he had plenty of company.

In 527 sorties that day (a sortie is one flight by a single military plane), Mitscher's pilots sank all four of Ozawa's carriers—*Chitose*, *Zuikaku*, *Chiyoda*, and *Zuiho*—and a destroyer. The Americans lost fewer than twenty aircraft. Just as Halsey's warships were on the verge of wiping out the rest of the Northern Force, he received distress calls from Admiral Kinkaid's 7th Fleet: "URGENTLY NEED BBS [battleships] LEYTE GULF AT ONCE."[86]

Kinkaid followed this message with two similarly urgent requests. But Halsey, in the middle of his own fight, believed his first duty was to destroy Ozawa's carriers and remained on station. The controversy surrounding Halsey's decision originated out of seemingly conflicting orders from the split MacArthur/Nimitz command.

Halsey's orders, agreed to by both Pacific commanders, stated that he was "to cover and support [MacArthur's] forces of Southwest Pacific in order to assist the seizure and occupation of objectives in the Central Philippines." But Nimitz's instructions to Halsey added the following proviso: "In case opportunity for destruction of major portion of the enemy fleet offers or can be created, such destruction becomes the primary task."[87] Halsey followed his last order first, as is customary in most military services, and for that was criticized for leaving MacArthur's landing forces exposed. The controversy still rages.

When Admiral Nimitz himself finally radioed Halsey requesting his whereabouts, Halsey swung about and commenced a three-hundred-mile race to the south, but it was too late to catch Kurita's Center Force. Halsey later declared that the gravest error he had made during the battle was "bowing to pressure and turning south."[88]

Action off Samar

That same morning, Admiral Kurita's Center Force had traversed the San Bernardino Strait and turned south, while Halsey's 3rd Fleet was attacking Ozawa to the north. Halsey, whose pursuit of Ozawa's carriers left the Leyte landing uncovered, had neglected to notify Admiral Kinkaid of his departure. Kurita's southward advance caught

Flying from the decks of Task Force 38 (left), Admiral Mitscher's Helldivers and Avengers sank all four of Admiral Ozawa's carriers, including the Zuikaku (below).

Rear Admiral Clifton A. F. Sprague's Task Unit 77.2.3—Taffy 3—by complete surprise. Sprague, with six escort carriers, three destroyers, and four destroyer escorts—armed only with five-inch guns—suddenly found himself locked in battle with Kurita's four battleships, six heavy cruisers, and some ten destroyers. Sprague, though overwhelmed, elected to fight. "If we can get this [Kurita's] task force to attack us," he said, "we can delay its descent on Leyte until help comes, though obviously the end will come sooner for us."[89]

Sprague laid down a smoke screen and drew his force into a rough circle reminiscent of the wagon trains of old and engaged Kurita in a remarkable running

---

Burning from a hit and bracketed by near misses, the escort carrier USS Gambier Bay *is seen here shortly before it was sunk.*

battle. Gamely fighting off extinction, Taffy 3 lost the CVE *Gambier Bay*, the DDs *Hoel* and *Johnston*, and the DE *Samuel B. Roberts*—and Kurita's ships were closing in for the kill. But in Taffy 3's moment of most urgent need, the cavalry arrived—planes from Taffy 1 and Taffy 2.

One torpedo-bomber pilot recalled that aircraft from Taffy 1, 2, and 3 started "hitting the [Japanese] ships with everything in the armory—including doorknobs."[90] When the Americans ran out of bombs and torpedoes, they refueled and returned to harass Kurita's ships with dummy runs.

Then, with victory within his grasp and perhaps only moments away, Kurita—thinking that he was being attacked by Admiral Mitscher's Task Force 38—turned his Center Force around and fled back through the San Bernardino Strait. Two of his cruisers—*Chikuma* and *Chokai*—remained off Samar, at the bottom of the Philippine Sea. Rear Admiral Clifton A. F. Sprague, in his after-action report, critiqued the fight off Samar this way:

The failure of the enemy . . . to wipe out all vessels of this task unit can be attributed to our successful smoke-screen, our torpedo counterattack, continuous harassment of the enemy by bomb, torpedo, and strafing air attacks, timely maneuvers, and the definite partiality of Almighty God.[91]

"Concentrated Attention"

On the last day of the Battle of Leyte Gulf, Emmet Crozier, staff correspondent of the New York *Herald Tribune,* telephoned his report of the classic naval encounter to his newspaper. The following is an excerpt of his report (as it appears in *Typewriter Battalion,* edited by Jack Stenbuck):

> PACIFIC FLEET HEADQUARTERS, Oct. 26, 1944—Japan has been reduced to a third-rate sea power and her entire defenses have been gravely impaired as a result of the disastrous naval defeat administered by United States fighting planes and ships in the Philippine Sea and the central Philippine area. . . .
>
> Here at Pacific Fleet Headquarters reports are still coming in on the last phase of the battle. Early yesterday our carrier aircraft and fast cruisers and battleships were still pursuing crippled remnants of the Japanese fleet. It was thought possible the score would be even larger when the final dispatches are analyzed.
>
> Summing up the practical results of the engagement, it may be said that the damage done to the Japanese ships remaining afloat exceeds the known repair capacity of the Japanese shipyards; and it may be added that the enemy repair facilities will receive concentrated attention in the near future.

The Final Tally

In the aftermath of the Samar fighting, Rear Admiral Thomas L. Sprague's escort carriers and Rear Admiral Jesse B. Oldendorf's warships, returning from the battle in Surigao Strait, were assaulted by land-based aircraft. The event introduced the first kamikaze attacks of the war. The enemy suicide pilots sank the CVE *St. Lô* and damaged several other ships.

The Battle of Leyte Gulf ended the next day, 26 October 1944, when American carrier planes sank another cruiser of Kurita's fleeing Center Force in the Sulu Sea. In the end, Japan utterly failed to prevent the American landings on Leyte, and the Imperial Japanese Navy did not come close to achieving victory in its "great decisive battle" with the U.S. Navy. The battle cost Japan more than 300,000 tons of warships—three battleships, four carriers, ten cruisers, and nine destroyers—and destroyed the IJN's ability to fight another naval battle.

The United States lost thirty-seven thousand tons of combat ships—one light and two escort carriers, two destroyers, and one destroyer escort. The way now stood open for the conquest of the Philippines and for islands closer to Japan—the first of which was Iwo Jima.

Chapter 6

Iwo Jima: Uncommon Valor

"When the capture of an enemy position is necessary to winning a war it is not within our province to evaluate the cost in money, time, equipment, or most of all, in human life. We are told what our objective is to be and we prepare to do the job."
—Lieutenant General Holland M. ("Howlin' Mad") Smith, (quoted in Paul M. Kennedy, "Iwo Jima (1945)" in *The Mammoth Book of Battles*, edited by Jon E. Lewis)

At 1020 on Friday, 23 February 1945, First Lieutenant Harold G. Schrier and five men of Company E, 2nd Battalion, 28th Marines, raised the American flag on the crest of Iwo Jima's Mount Suribachi. Lieutenant Colonel Chandler W. Johnson, their battalion commander, recognizing the historical significance of the moment, wanted to preserve the flag. That afternoon he sent a larger flag to the mountain's crest to replace the original American colors.

When the second flag was raised atop Suribachi at 1430 by five other marines and a navy corpsman, Associated Press photographer Joe Rosenthal snapped the picture that was destined to become the most famous war photograph ever taken—later reproduced on a postage stamp and immortalized as a giant memorial statue at Arlington National Cemetery. After the second flag-raising, the men of the 28th Marine Regiment and the 5th Engineer Battalion set about the business of demolishing 165 concrete pillboxes and sealing 200 caves used for living, fighting, and storage. The fighting for Iwo Jima had only just begun.

Iwo

Iwo Jima, a pork-chop-shaped flyspeck of an island only 5.5 miles long by 2.5 miles wide, lies 759 miles south of Tokyo. The

Marines raise the second American flag atop Mount Suribachi, 23 February 1945.

center island of three in the Volcano Islands, it is sulfurous (its name means Sulfur Island), volcanic, ugly, smelly, and waterless—but strategically located halfway between Japan and the Marianas. Until 19 February 1945, the day that U.S. Marines commenced landing on the barren speck of black sand and ash, most Americans had never heard of it. Now it is recognized by millions of people—not only in the United States but around the world—as the setting for one of the fiercest battles ever fought on planet Earth.

The Americans wanted Iwo Jima for a number of reasons, principally, to deny Japan the use of its airfields; to provide

emergency landing fields for B-29s bombing Japan and for shorter-range fighters escorting the Superfortresses; and for the dispiriting psychological effect on the Japanese that its loss would produce. The Japanese were not blind to Iwo Jima's importance and began reinforcing its garrison and shoring up its defenses in October 1944.

The Japanese Army high command sent Lieutenant General Tadamichi Kuribayashi to Iwo to command a garrison of some twenty thousand men, with orders to hold out as long as possible. A fifty-four-year-old former cavalry officer and commander of the Emperor's Imperial Guard, Kuribayashi packed two hundred pounds on a 5'9" frame. Lest anyone view his ample midsection as a sign of weakness or lack of will, Radio Tokyo described him as one whose "partly protruding belly is packed full of strong fighting spirit."[92]

The marines who were about to challenge that image would soon come to view Kuribayashi as "the most redoubtable commander we faced in the entire war."[93]

By early 1945, Kuribayashi presided over a rocky island bastion unsurpassed by any other eight-square-mile fortification anywhere. His savage moonscape of sulfuric rock contained 360 completed pillboxes, deeply interconnected by caves and tunnels. This defensive network was nearly impervious to bombs and naval gunfire and bristled with a huge array of armament: 120 big guns larger than 75 millimeters; 300 antiaircraft guns larger than 25 millimeters; 20,000 small guns, including machine guns; 40 47-millimeters and 20 37-millimeters antitank guns; and 27 tanks.

All this added up to the costliest battle in the history of the Marine Corps. Of the eighty marines awarded the Medal of Honor during World War II, twenty-two earned it here. This was Iwo.

Questions

In a letter to his son, General Kuribayashi called Iwo Jima "the gateway to Japan."[94]

The old samurai knew that he and his island garrison were doomed. But he intended to keep the gates closed to the Americans as long as there was a single bullet left to be fired and a single Japanese warrior left to fire it. The Americans anticipated a tough fight, and the Japanese validated their expectations.

Admiral Chester W. Nimitz assigned the most able of his available commanders and his most experienced assault troops to open the gates to Tokyo. He entrusted overall control of the Iwo Jima operation to

Admiral Chester W. Nimitz (left) entrusted overall control of the Iwo Jima campaign to Vice Admiral Raymond A. Spruance (right).

Vice Admiral Raymond A. Spruance and his 5th Fleet, by then the most powerful naval force in the world. Spruance's role would be to provide distant cover against enemy air or sea attack and to participate in the air and naval preinvasion bombardment of Iwo. To head up the landing operations, Nimitz again chose Rear Admiral Richmond Kelly Turner, the war's most experienced amphibious operations commander.

Major General Harry Schmidt's V Amphibious Corps—some eighty-four thousand men in all, but primarily the 3rd, 4th, and 5th Marine Divisions—provided the assault troops. The 3rd Division (3rd, 9th, and 21st Marine Regiments), commanded by Major General Groves B. Erskine, had fought at Bougainville and Guam. Major General Clifton B. Cates's 4th Division (23rd, 24th, and 25th Marine Regiments) had seen action at Saipan and Tinian. Although Major General Keller E. Rockey's 5th Division (26th, 27th, and 28th Marine Regiments) had yet to see combat, it was well trained and staffed by many veterans. As commander of the Fleet Marine Force, Pacific, Lieutenant General Holland B. ("Howlin' Mad") Smith accompanied the invasion forces in the somewhat superfluous role of commanding general, expeditionary forces.

Given the high quality of leadership and the unrivaled caliber of fighting troops, no American combatant at Iwo held the slightest doubt about the success of the invasion. On the eve of battle, the questions that begged answers were how long would it take and at what cost?

Black Ash, Blood, and an Unseen Foe

D day at Iwo was set for Monday, 19 February 1945. After three weeks of intensive aerial bombardment and three days of naval shelling, the first attack waves of the 4th and 5th Marine Divisions churned ashore in every manner of landing craft available—LCIs, Higgins boats, LSMs, LSTs, LVTs, and more. "At dawn on D-Day," wrote eyewitness John P. Marquand of *Harper's* magazine, "the waters of Iwo Jima looked like New York harbor on a busy day."[95]

Fifth Amphibious Corps commander Major General Harry Schmidt's simple plan called for the marines to take the airfields (two operational and one under construction) as soon as possible, seize 550-foot-high Mount Suribachi on Iwo's southern end, and then combine all forces and drive north. Lieutenant General Tadamichi Kuribayashi's battle plan was simpler yet, calling for "a gradual depletion of the enemy's attack forces, and even if the situation gets out of hand, defend a corner of the island to the death."[96]

At 0859, the first marines hit the beach, a sloping terrace of volcanic ash eight to fifteen feet high—high enough to cut off their fields of fire. One Japanese officer, watching from his Suribachi cave, observed, "At nine o'clock in the morning, several hundred landing craft with amphibious

As sulfurous gases rise from Suribachi, marines of the first assault wave crawl up the black ashen beach of Iwo Jima.

tanks in the lead rushed ashore like an enormous tidal wave."[97] Eight thousand marines poured ashore in the first few minutes.

From left to right (south to north), the seven assault beaches were designated Green, Red 1 and 2, Yellow 1 and 2, and Blue 1 and 2. They were all black. Following Kuribayashi's orders, his disciplined troops deliberately held their fire for about fifteen minutes, until the beaches were swarming with marines—Rockey's 5th Division on the left, Cates's 4th on the right. Then, suddenly, every Japanese gun, howitzer, and mortar on the island opened fire on the exposed marines.

Lieutenant Colonel Justice Chambers, who led his 25th Marines up the sheer face of the "Rock Quarry" on the right flank, commented on the murderous fire. "You could've held up a cigarette and lit it on the stuff going by," he said "I knew we were in for one hell of a time."[98]

Unlike Tarawa, there was no sheltering seawall—only black volcanic ash. Kuribayashi's artillery and small-arms fire, plus hundreds of land mines buried in the black sand and ash of the beaches, took a frightful toll of men and machines that first day. Twenty-four hundred marines were hit, including six hundred dead. Even so, Rockey's 5th Division troops fought their way across the narrow neck of the "pork chop," at the base of Mount Suribachi, and isolated the southern defense forces. Meanwhile, Cates's 4th Division marines nailed down the right flank of V Amphibious Corps. But neither division gained their first-day objectives.

At day's end, the marines dug in, expecting the routine banzai (suicide) counterattack in the name of the emperor, to which so many of them had become accustomed. ("Banzai" is a form of greeting given to their emperor meaning ten thousand years [of life to you].) No wild, screaming attacks came, but artillery and mortar fire from an unseen enemy continued to screech down on the marines all night.

Guts

On Tuesday, their second day ashore, the 28th Marines drove forward to the base of

Suribachi in a light rain. Its bleak, gray mountainside contained sixteen hundred Japanese, solidly entrenched in well-concealed pillboxes, bunkers, caves, and spider holes (foxholes linked together to form a defensive network or web). Picking their way slowly, addressing each enemy strong point with grenades and demolitions, the marines had advanced two hundred yards by dark and sealed off forty caves used as defensive installations. To their right, or behind them, the 26th and 27th Marines had reached the west coast of the island and the southern end of Airfield No. 1 and were pressing northward.

In the meantime, the 23rd, 24th, and 25th Marines of Cates's 4th Division, their left flank at the airport and their right secured to the cliff area bordering the eastern beach, were also advancing to the north.

By noon Wednesday, the 1st and 3rd Battalions of the 28th Marines reached the base of Suribachi. By dark, they had the mountain surrounded. Offshore that same day, fifty kamikazes struck the U.S. invasion fleet, severely damaging the fleet carrier *Saratoga* and sinking the escort carrier *Bismarck Sea.*

At first, General Erskine's 3rd Division remained in floating reserve. General Holland

Smith and Admiral Kelly Turner hoped that Erskine's troops would not be needed on Iwo and instead held for the invasion of Okinawa, next on the Allied agenda. But their hopes did not materialize.

After only forty-eight hours, the 3rd Division's 21st Marines were sent into action in a hot spot the marines dubbed "the Wilderness"—an area inland from Blue Beach 2 that covered about a square mile on the approaches to Airfield No. 2. They

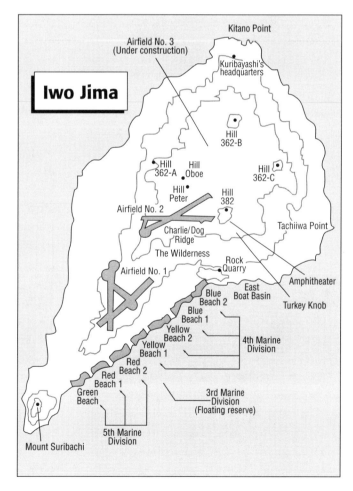

were ordered "to advance at all costs." In the Wilderness, wrote one Marine Corps combat correspondent,

> There was no cover. Here and there stood a blasted dwarf tree; here and there a stubby rock ledge in a maze of volcanic crevices. . . .

> Behind a rolling artillery barrage and with fixed bayonets, the unit leaped forward in an old-fashioned hell-bent-for-leather charge and advanced to the very mouth of the fixed Jap defenses. Before scores of pillboxes the men flung themselves at the tiny flaming holes, throwing grenades and jabbing with bayonets. Comrades went past, hurdled the defenses and rushed across Airfield No. 2. In three minutes one unit lost four officers. Men died at every step. That was how we broke their line.[99]

This kind of action was typical of the courage and spirit of self-sacrifice exhibited by the marines all across Iwo; this was how they achieved on foot what aerial bombardment, naval shelling, artillery, and tanks had been unable to accomplish in two days of incessant pounding.

The Way They Did It

Mount Suribachi fell to the 28th Marines on 23 February, the fifth day of fighting. When the marines unfurled Old Glory on its summit, Secretary of the Navy James V. Forrestal, watching at the base of the mountain, turned to General Howlin' Mad Smith and said, "Holland, the raising of that flag on Suribachi means a Marine Corps for the next 500 years."[100] (Forrestal's remark alluded to critics of the Marine Corps who had been questioning the need for an amphibious assault force.) Few marines on Iwo Jima were looking that far ahead.

The 5th Marine Division now turned 180 degrees from Mount Suribachi and attacked up the west coast of the island, while the 4th Division advanced up the east coast. General Erskine came ashore with the rest of his division that day. The 3rd Division occupied the center of the three-division line the next day and struck north across Airfield No. 2. In five days of fighting, the marines had absorbed more than six thousand casualties, including sixteen hundred dead, but they now owned the entire southern third of Iwo Jima.

With the marines driving northward toward the menacing lines of pillboxes and bunkers that guarded Iwo's northern plateau, General Kuribayashi issued his last order:

> We shall infiltrate into the midst of the enemy and annihilate them. We shall grasp bombs, charge the enemy tanks and destroy them. With every salvo we will, without fail, kill the enemy. Each man will make it his duty to kill ten of the enemy before dying.[101]

Only 2,630 yards of island remained to be taken, but the cost in human sacrifice became immeasurable. As the second phase of the fighting commenced against Kuribayashi's main defenses on the Motoyama Plateau, pressure soon mounted on the American commanders to end the fighting quickly. The U.S. fleet had to be freed for the invasion of Okinawa, now set for 1 April 1945. But some things take time—plus, as in the case of securing Iwo Jima, a huge measure of courage. In the official history of the 4th Division, one lieutenant writes:

> It takes courage for officers to send their men ahead, when many they've known since the division came into existence are already gone. It takes courage to crawl ahead, 100 yards a day, and get up the next morning, count losses and do it again. But that's the only way it can be done.[102]

And that's the way the marines did it—a few yards at a time, a few lives at a time—relentlessly inching forward.

On a daily basis, the marines bayoneted, knifed, blasted, flamed, and ultimately routed a determined enemy from their rock-solid defensive positions. They attacked, attacked, attacked, overrunning and overcoming their foe in such aptly nicknamed places as the "Meat Grinder" and "Bloody Gorge," plus countless lethal ridges, crevices, and caves. In the final tally, they took more casualties than they gave. But that was the only way it could be done.

Reporting on the Dead and Wounded

In "The First Three Days," an article written for *Life* (3 March 1945) and reprinted in part 2 of the Library of America's *Reporting World War II,* intrepid war correspondent Robert Sherrod reports on Iwo Jima's dead and wounded:

> About the dead, whether Jap or American, there was one thing in common. They died with the greatest possible violence. Nowhere in the Pacific War have I seen such badly mangled bodies. Many were cut squarely in half. Legs and arms lay 50 feet away from any body. In one spot on the sand, far from the nearest cluster of dead men, I saw a string of guts 15 feet long. There are 250 wounded aboard the transport where this story is being written. One of the doctors tells me that 90% of them require major surgery. Off Normandy last summer, he says, only 5% who were brought aboard this transport needed such surgery. On the beach this morning I saw at least 50 men still fighting despite their wounds. Only the incapacitated request evacuation.

Wounded in the face, a marine awaits treatment aboard a transport.

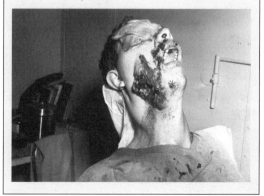

"Thank God for the Marines!"

The marines cracked Kuribayashi's main defensive belt across the central highlands on 4 March, a date that unexpectedly marked a second important event that afternoon: The B-29 Superfortress *Dinah Might*, crippled in a raid over Tokyo, limped into the island's still fire-swept bomber strip for an emergency landing. Cheers rang out from every marine foxhole. One marine shouted, "That's why we are here!"[103] The *Dinah Might*, repaired and refueled, took off amid enemy fire thirty minutes later and headed back to its base in the Marianas. It was the first of twenty-four hundred American bombers that would make an emergency landing on Iwo Jima by the end of the war.

On 9 March, General Erskine's 3rd Division drove through to the sea at the north end of the island. General Cates's 4th Division crushed the last enemy resistance on the east coast a week later. The 5th Division fought on until 26 March, however, before General Rockey could report all enemy opposition eliminated on the west coast.

On the last day of fighting, General Kuribayashi burned his colors and readied himself for death. At nightfall, he led some five hundred thirsty and starved survivors in a last banzai attack on the Americans. The fighting lasted for hours. In the morning, several hundred American bodies lay entangled with five hundred Japanese corpses. Among them lay the unidentified body of Kuribayashi, a seventh-generation samurai who chose to die fighting.

Damaged in a raid over Japan, a B-29 makes an emergency landing on Iwo Jima and crashes into a parked fighter plane.

The marine cemetery on Iwo Jima. During the battle, the Marine Corps suffered the highest casualty rate in its history.

The battle for Iwo Jima cost the U.S. Marines almost 20,000 wounded and 6,821 dead. Of some 20,000 Japanese defenders, only 216 survived. In the fiercest fighting of the Pacific War so far, the marines suffered an appalling casualty rate of 1.25 to 1, the highest in the history of the Marine Corps.

In ringing tribute to the Americans who bore the battle on Iwo Jima, Admiral Nimitz later wrote, "Among the Americans who served on Iwo Island, uncommon valor was a common virtue."[104] The admiral's words are now chiseled into the base of the huge statue in Arlington National Cemetery commemorating the Suribachi flag raisers.

After the fighting ended on Iwo Jima, a crew member of one of the many shot-up B-29s that emergency-landed safely there put it another way, no less sincere. "Thank God for the Marines!"[105] he said.

★ Chapter 7 ★

Okinawa: The Last Battle

"One plane for one warship. One boat for one ship. One man for ten enemy. One man for one tank."

—Creed of the Japanese 32nd Army on Okinawa (quoted in Norman Polmar and Thomas B. Allen, *World War II: The Encyclopedia of the War Years 1941–1945*)

Operation Iceberg, the massive, complex, and bloody invasion of Okinawa, commenced at 0406 on Easter Sunday morning, 1 April 1945. It began with a hush. Soldiers and marines who splashed ashore on L day (Landing Day) met with so little resistance that the Americans dubbed it "Love Day." Assault troops of the 1st and 6th Marine Divisions, many of them veterans accustomed to more fiery receptions in earlier Pacific campaigns, encountered only minor skirmishes.

On the second day ashore, Major General Pedro Del Valle, commander of the 1st Marine Division, called a press conference and said, "I don't know where the Japs are, and I can't offer any good reason why they let us come ashore so easily. We're pushing

on across the island as fast as we can move the men and equipment."[106]

When the calm continued for several more days, "Love Day turned into Honeymoon Week on Okinawa,"[107] recalled Robert Leckie, military historian and former marine. But as with most honeymoons, it ended all too soon.

Joint Venture

Preparations for Operation Iceberg began in September 1944, when the U.S. Joint Chiefs of Staff decided that Okinawa, rather than Formosa or the Philippines, would serve as the springboard for the final invasion of Japan. Okinawa is an island group centered in the Ryukyu Island chain, which comprises the large island of

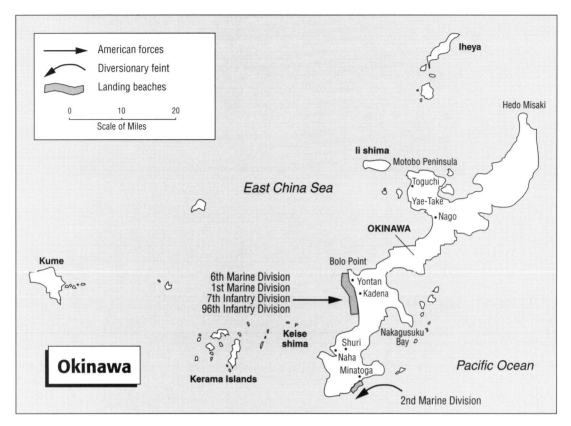

Okinawa and the smaller islands of Ii shima (Ie shima), Iheya, Kume, and the Kerama Islands. The 70-mile long large island of Okinawa lies 340 miles south of mainland Japan, about halfway between Kyushu and Formosa, with the East China Sea to the west and the Pacific Ocean to the east. Its entirely coral formation covers approximately 454 square miles.

Okinawa stood as the last Japanese island bastion short of the Japanese home islands themselves. The Americans considered its capture vital to their projected invasion of Japan proper (Kyushu in November 1945, Honshu in March 1946), partly be-

cause it contained several air bases and partly because ownership of the island would sever Japan's sea access to its forces in China. The Japanese, well aware that Okinawa was equally vital to their survival, assigned its defense to Lieutenant General Mitsuru Ushijima and his 32nd Army, some 130,000-men strong (including about 20,000 Okinawan militia).

Ushijima planned to engage the American invaders in a protracted defensive mode, selling the life of each of his men at as high a cost as possible. Shunning the tenets of Bushido, the warrior's code, he exhorted his troops:

You cannot regard the enemy on a par with you. You must realize that material power usually overcomes spiritual power in the present war. The enemy is clearly superior in machines. Do not depend on your spirits overcoming the enemy. Devise combat methods based on mathematical precision: then think about your spiritual power.[108]

In short, Ushijima's philosophy seemed to say, "Make each life last for as long as possible and trade it for as much as possible—and forget false heroics."

To overcome still another anticipated strong Japanese defense, Admiral Chester W. Nimitz again called on Vice Admiral Raymond A. Spruance's 5th Fleet to provide striking power and protection for Rear Admiral Richmond Kelly Turner's landing force, now called the Joint Expeditionary Force (JEF). Vice Admiral Marc A. Mitscher's fast carrier attack force (Task Force 58) sought control of the skies, complemented by several British warships (Task Force 57) led by Vice Admiral H. B. Rawlings. Mitscher's task was not an enviable one. It included guarding the entire fleet against attacks from land-based planes on Formosa and Kyushu, including kamikazes—

the use of which the Japanese had now committed themselves to—and providing air cover for the ground forces ashore. Admiral Turner commanded the actual amphibious operations. The invasion fleet was the largest of the Pacific War, containing 1,213 warships and auxiliary vessels.

At the insistence of the War Department, Lieutenant General Simon Bolivar Buckner, U.S. Army, replaced Lieutenant

Struck by antiaircraft fire, a kamikaze dives toward an escort carrier. During the battle for Okinawa, the suicide pilots would maul Task Force 58.

General Holland M. Smith, U.S. Marine Corps, as shore commander of the newly created U.S. 10th Army. The 10th Army consisted of the 3rd Marine Amphibious Corps (the 1st and 6th Marine Divisions, with the 2nd in reserve) under Major General Roy S. Geiger and the 24th Army Corps (the 7th, 77th, and 96th Infantry Divisions, with the 27th in reserve) commanded by Major General John R. Hodge. In all, Buckner's force totaled 182,112 men. British observers called this joint U.S. Army–Navy–Marine Corps operation "the most audacious and complex enterprise yet undertaken by American amphibious forces."[109] It was also one of the costliest.

The Battle Heats Up

In preliminary air operations (14–31 March 1945), Admiral Mitscher's carrier aircraft, Admiral Rawlings's British carrier force, and U.S. land-based bombers attacked Japanese air bases from Honshu to Formosa to isolate Okinawa from hostile air attacks. These strikes temporarily paralyzed Japanese air operations over and off the battle zone and destroyed 169 of 193 kamikazes committed to the action, but not before Mitscher's carriers took a beating. The kamikazes crippled the *Franklin* so badly that it had to be towed out of action by the cruiser *Pittsburgh*. The *Wasp* and the *Yorktown* were also severely damaged, but newly developed fire-fighting techniques saved all three carriers.

Preliminary bombardment of Okinawa began a week before the main invasion. On

26 March, the U.S. 77th Infantry Division (24th Corps) occupied the Kerama Islands, west of Okinawa, to preempt a force of Japanese suicide boats and establish an anchorage for the invasion fleet. On the main island, underwater demolition teams (UDTs or frogmen) destroyed a complex tangle of beach obstacles and cleared the way for the landings.

The invasion fleet now moved into position and stood off the Hagushi beaches on the west side of Okinawa. The melodic tones of Tokyo Rose (a U.S. citizen who broadcast Japanese propaganda) could be heard chiding the Americans:

> This is the Zero Hour, boys. It is broadcast for all you American fighting men in the Pacific, particularly those standing off the shores of Okinawa . . . because many of you will never hear another program. . . . Here's a good number, "Going Home" . . . it's nice work if you can get it. . . . You boys off Okinawa listen and enjoy it while you can, because when you're dead you're a long time dead. . . . Let's have a little jukebox music for the boys and make it hot. . . . The boys are going to catch hell soon, and they might as well get used to the heat.[110]

Tokyo Rose purred on, describing a host of unpleasant deaths awaiting the Americans ashore. But the marines and GIs landed on the Hagushi beaches to a cool reception—the 1st and 6th Marine Divisions to the

"Those Who've Been There"

"Perhaps the greatest tribute to the American fighting men on Okinawa came from their favorite English-language broadcaster, Radio Tokyo [Tokyo Rose]," writes military historian Robert Leckie in *Okinawa*. This is the tribute:

Tokyo Rose.

Sugar Loaf Hill . . . Chocolate Drop . . . Strawberry Hill. Gee, these places sound wonderful! You can just see the candy houses with the white picket fences around them and the candy canes hanging from the trees, their red and white stripes glistening in the sun. But the only thing red about these places is the blood of Americans. Yes, sir, these are the names of hills in southern Okinawa where the fighting's so close that you can get down to bayonets and sometimes your bare fists. . . . I guess it's natural to idealize the worst places with pretty names to make them seem less awful. Why, Sugar Loaf has changed hands so often it looks like Dante's Inferno. Yes, sir, Sugar Loaf Hill . . . Chocolate Drop . . . Strawberry Hill. They sound good, don't they? Only those who've been there know what they're really like.

north, the 7th and 96th Infantry Divisions to their south. They landed in eight successive waves, under cover of air and naval bombardment, and proceeded to take care of business.

The marines of Geiger's 3rd Amphibious Corps turned north and encountered only token resistance, clearing the entire northern end of the island by 13 April. The marines' toughest fighting came at Mount Yae Take, on the Motobu Peninsula in the north. It took the 6th Marine Division five

days to clear the twelve-hundred-foot-high mountain, with a big assist from the sea and air forces. Afterward, division operations officer Lieutenant Colonel Victor ("Brute") Krulak explained, "They weren't going anywhere—they were going to fight to the death."[111] The marines obliged more than 2,000 of their enemy, while taking almost 1,000 casualties of their own—207 killed, 752 wounded, and 6 missing.

A week later, the newly committed 77th Infantry Division secured the offshore island of Ii shima (20 April) after four days of hard fighting, killing 4,700 of the enemy. American losses were 258 dead and 879 wounded. The dead included Ernie Pyle, the renowned war correspondent, a victim of a Japanese machine-gun bullet. Soldier-cartoonist Bill Mauldin, noted for his portrayals of archetypal combat infantrymen Willie and Joe, said of Pyle's passing, "The only difference between Ernie's death and that of any other good guy is that the other guy is mourned by his company. Ernie is mourned by the Army."[112]

In the meantime, to the south, Hodge's advancing 24th Corps slammed into Ushijima's Machinato Line and was stopped in its tracks on 4 April. The line stretched from Naha on the west coast, through Shuri, to Yonabaru on the east coast. It formed the Japanese first line of resistance in the southern Shuri Zone—a heavily fortified, interlocking system of caves, bunkers, and tunnels, with big guns mounted on tracks so that they could be rolled out of caves and back in to avoid return fire. One veteran later characterized the deeply dug defensive network as looking "like ships inside hills."[113] While General Buckner sought ways to

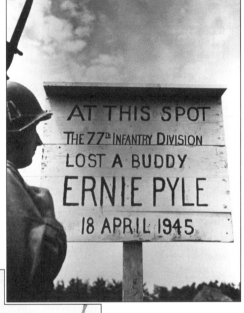

Marines of the 3rd Marine Amphibious Corps attempt to break through the Machinato Line (left). On the island of Ii shima, soldiers erected a monument to fallen war correspondent Ernie Pyle (above).

penetrate Ushijima's defenses, kamikazes were dropping like rain on ships of the Allied fleet offshore. Operation Iceberg was heating up.

Heavenly Operation

The Japanese High Command, convinced that kamikaze attacks offered the only effective means of countering the powerful Allied fleet at Okinawa, launched *Ten-Go*, or Heavenly Operation, an Okinawa defense plan developed at the start of 1945. The plan's two principal elements were (1) a joint army-navy all-out air attack on the Allied invasion fleet, employing more than four thousand aircraft, both suicide and conventional, and (2) a desperation attack by Japan's few remaining warships, including the superbattleship *Yamato*, with orders to battle to the death—without air cover.

Although dates are often arbitrary, *Ten-Go* essentially began on 6 April, with a massive attack by kamikazes called *kikusui* (floating chrysanthemums). According to aviation historian and archivist Walter J. Boyne, "In just a few minutes, 476 chrysanthemums floated no more."[114] But 180 kamikazes got through to their targets in the forty-eight-hour-long attack, sinking four warships and damaging nineteen more. Nine more large-scale and untold smaller attacks followed between then and 22 June.

While the Allied fleet battled kamikazes off Okinawa, U.S. carrier planes attacked and sank the *Yamato*, along with a cruiser and four destroyers, steaming south in the East China Sea to join the fray. Writes battle historian David Eggenberger,

The battleship *Yamato narrowly avoids a bomb dropped by an American plane off Okinawa. Navy bombers and torpedo planes would soon sink her.*

> The Nippon navy was virtually extinct. Japanese aircraft assaulted the Tenth Army and its offshore shipping throughout the land battle. Bombers did little damage, but in some 1,900 attacks *kamikazes* dived through air defenses to sink 36 U.S. ships and damage another 368. These attacks killed 4,907 navy men and wounded another 4,824. But during the three-month battle some 7,800 Japanese planes were destroyed, at a cost of 763 U.S. aircraft. Japanese air power had become a shadow.[115]

For all concerned, the Heavenly Operation turned out to be emphatically hellish.

A Major Mistake

Back ashore, General Buckner's 24th Corps kept banging away at the Machinato Line and, aided by the 1st and 6th Marine and 77th Infantry Divisions, finally pierced it on 24 April, only to be stopped short again at the Shuri Line, Ushijima's main line of resistance. Buckner then faced a dilemma: With the 1st and 6th Marine and 77th Infantry Divisions idle and available, he could press them into service along a compacted front of barely nine thousand yards or he could, as the marines urged, launch an amphibious attack to Ushijima's rear to end the campaign quickly. Buckner opted for a more conventional double envelopment—frontal attacks penetrating both flanks (rather than a preemptive amphibious strike to the rear). He reorganized on a two-corps front, deploying the marines on the right (west).

Marine leaders and some army critics felt that Buckner erred on the side of caution. In an interview after the war, Japanese senior operations officer Colonel Hiromichi Yahara commented, "The absence of a landing puzzled the 32nd Army staff, particularly after the beginning of May when it became impossible to put up more than a token resistance in the south."[116] It was at this point that General Ushijima committed a major mistake: Against Yahara's advice, he launched a counterattack.

"To take the offensive with inferior forces against overwhelming superior enemy forces is reckless and will lead to early defeat,"[117] Yahara argued. Ushijima did not listen. Instead, on 3–4 May, he hurled his 24th Division—backed by artillery, tanks, and a kamikaze attack from Kyushu—against the U.S. 7th Infantry Division on his right (east) flank. At the same time, he struck with a minor attack against the 1st Marine Division on his western flank. American troops, artillery, tactical air strikes, and naval gunfire chopped the attackers to pieces. When the smoke lifted, Ushijima's counterattack was crushed and some 5,000 Japanese soldiers lay dead. Buckner lost 1,066 casualties. The failed assault also revealed the locations of Ushijima's previously hidden artillery.

The Imminence of Doom

A week later, General Buckner launched his own offensive. Despite heavy spring rains and fierce enemy resistance, his troops pressed steadily into and around Ushijima's Shuri Line. On 23 May, the 6th Marine Division—after some of the bitterest fighting of the campaign on Sugar Loaf Hill and two adjacent hills—crossed the Asato River and swarmed into Naha, then proceeded to turn the left flank of the Japanese line. Describing one day's fighting on Sugar Loaf Hill, 22nd Marine squad leader Corporal James Day later said:

> The real danger at Sugar Loaf was not the hill itself where we were, but in a 300-yard-by-300-yard killing zone which

the Marines had to cross. . . . It was a dismal sight, men falling, tanks getting knocked out. . . . The division probably suffered 600 casualties that day. [118]

Corporal Day, the last man in his squad, survived the war and returned to Okinawa forty years later, as Major General James Day, commanding all Marine Corps installations on the island.

Six days later, the 1st Marine Division, after more of the same kind of fighting, overran the Shuri hill mass in the center of the Shuri Line. At the same time, the 24th Corps turned Ushijima's right flank and pressed steadily forward down the eastern side of the island. The Japanese now began a slow, fighting withdrawal into the hills at the island's southern tip.

On 4 June, the 6th Marine Division mounted a shore-to-shore amphibious assault on the Oroku Peninsula, in the southwest, conquering it after another ten days of savage fighting. The 8th Marines of the 2nd Marine Division, summoned from Saipan, now joined Buckner's main thrust to the southern tip of the island, a two-pronged army-marine attack around and over the remnants of Ushijima's 32nd Army.

On 17 June, General Buckner sent an air-dropped message to General Ushijima. It said, in part:

The forces under your command have fought bravely and well, and your infantry tactics have merited the respect of your opponents. . . . Like myself, you are an infantry general long schooled and practiced in infantry warfare. You fully know the pitiful plight of your defense forces. You know that no reinforcements can reach you. I believe, therefore, that you understand as clearly as I that destruction of all Japanese resistance on the island is merely a matter of days, and that this will entail the necessity of my killing the vast majority of your remaining troops.[119]

Ushijima held no thoughts of surrender, however, and as fate would have it, he outlived his would-be benefactor. The next day, Lieutenant General Simon Bolivar Buckner, while observing the 8th Marines at the battlefront, was struck by shrapnel from an artillery round and died ten minutes later. Major General Roy S. Geiger succeeded him, marking the first time in the nation's history that a marine commanded an army in combat.

On 21 June, the 10th Army reached the southern tip of the island and turned back to begin mopping-up operations. The next day, before the Americans reached his cave, Lieutenant General Mitsuru Ushijima knelt and slit open his abdomen. "The Okinawans must resent me,"[120] he said. An aide severed his spinal column. The aide and six others then shot themselves.

Later, at Kadena Airfield, the Americans held a flag-raising ceremony, while a 10th Army band played the national anthem. After eighty-three days, the Okinawa

Gratitude

In *The Battle for Okinawa*, Colonel Hiromichi Yahara, the chief of operations on the island, includes this telegram of commendation received on Okinawa from Imperial Headquarters on 20 June 1945:

> Under command of Lieutenant General Mitsuru Ushijima, you have fought courageously for three months against a formidable enemy, ever since his landing on Okinawa. You have destroyed the enemy in every battlefield, causing great damage. You have truly displayed the greatness of the Imperial Army. In addition you have restrained the enemy's overwhelming naval power. You have also contributed greatly to our air raids against enemy fleets.

Yahara drafted this reply:

> Against the overwhelmingly powerful enemy, with our survivors at hand, as we are about to make an all-out suicide attack, we received the commendation bestowed by your excellency. Nothing can surpass this glory. We are supremely moved. The soldiers who have died shedding their blood on these islands of Okinawa can now rest in peace forever. The remaining soldiers at this final stand are encouraged to fight to the death. With all our strength we will fight bravely so that we will come up to your expectations. We are very grateful.

Lieutenant General Mitsuru Ushijima. Imperial Headquarters commended his chief of operations, Colonel Hiromichi Yahara, for the courageous defense of Okinawa.

campaign was over, and the last battle of the war ended.

Okinawa was brutal and costly for both sides. The Japanese lost 107,500 known dead and probably thousands more sealed in caves. Army dead numbered 4,675; wounded, 18,099. Marine casualties totaled 2,938 dead and 13,708 wounded. Navy dead exceeded both the army and marines at 4,907, owing mostly to the effectiveness of the kamikazes. Navy wounded numbered 4,824. The Americans, at high cost, had secured the last stepping-stone to Japan. And the Japanese now felt the imminence of doom.

★ Epilogue ★

The Atomic Age and Beyond

The army, navy, and marine veterans of the island campaigns in the Pacific—New Guinea, Leyte, Luzon, Saipan, Peleliu, Iwo Jima, and all the rest—had survived to anticipate and prepare for the biggest and potentially bloodiest invasion of them all: the Japanese home islands. Under General Douglas MacArthur's direction, General Walter Krueger, now winding up his U.S. 6th Army's campaign in the Philippines, was already drawing up invasion plans for Kyushu in November 1945 (Operation Olympic) and Honshu in March 1946 (Operation Coronet). The two operations, labeled DOWNFALL, were to be executed by Krueger and his 6th Army, which would comprise eleven army divisions and three marine divisions. But DOWNFALL became unnecessary in light of later events in Washington.

The enormous cost in lives of the Iwo Jima and Okinawa operations, plus the potential for the deaths of hundreds of thousands more on both sides posed by the invasion of Japan, caused President Truman and the Joint Chiefs of Staff to reconsider their options. They decided to abandon invasion plans for Japan.

On 6 August 1945, the United States exploded an atomic bomb on the Japanese city of Hiroshima, and it dropped a second atomic bomb on Nagasaki three days later. Colonel Paul Tibbets, USAAF, commander of the *Enola Gay*—the B-29 Superfortress that dropped the atomic bomb on Hiroshima—described the event like this:

> There was the mushroom cloud growing up, and we watched it blossom. And down below it the thing reminded me more of a boiling pot of tar than any other description I can give it. It was black and boiling underneath with a steam haze on top of it.[121]

Almost 100,000 people died instantly. Another 35,000 died at Nagasaki. And thus the world entered the atomic age.

A White House statement released a few hours after the first atomic event revealed the existence of the horrendous new weapon. It cautioned that if the Japanese did not surrender, "they may expect a rain of ruin from the air, the like of which has never been seen on this earth."[122]

Japanese forces throughout Asia and the Pacific laid down their arms on 15 August. On 2 September 1945, General Douglas MacArthur accepted Japan's unconditional surrender aboard the U.S. battleship *Missouri* in Tokyo Bay, officially ending the greatest war in history.

General Douglas MacArthur signs the documents accepting Japan's surrender. Recently liberated from a Japanese prison camp, General Jonathan W. Wainright stands behind him.

Almost as a postscript to World War II, the Soviet Union declared war against Japan on 8 August 1945. This, among other spoils of war, afforded the Russians the right to occupy the northern half of Korea, which, in turn, led to the partitioning of Korea and the establishment of a Soviet puppet regime in North Korea. The seeds of two more wars had thus been planted—a cold war in Europe and a hot war in Korea.

☆ Notes ☆

Introduction: Selection of Battles

1. Quoted in John Toland, *The Rising Sun: The Decline and Fall of the Japanese Empire 1936–1945.* Vol. 1. New York: Random House, 1970, p. 390.
2. Frank O. Hough, "Action at Guadalcanal, 'Island of Death,' " in *Reader's Digest Illustrated Story of World War II.* Pleasantville, NY: Reader's Digest Association, 1978, p. 226.
3. Quoted in J. Robert Moskin, *The Story of the U.S. Marine Corps.* New York: Paddington Press, 1979, p. 304.
4. Quoted in Thomas J. Cutler, *The Battle of Leyte Gulf 23–26 October 1944.* New York: HarperCollins, 1994, p. 283.
5. Quoted in Richard Wheeler, *A Special Valor: The U.S. Marines and the Pacific War.* New York: Harper & Row, 1983, p. 383.
6. Quoted in Raymond Lamont-Brown, *Kamikaze: Japan's Suicide Samurai.* London: Arms & Armour Press, 1997, p. 64.

Chapter 1: World War II in the Pacific

7. Quoted in Gordon W. Prange, with Donald M. Goldstein and Katherine V. Dillon, *At Dawn We Slept: The Untold Story of Pearl Harbor.* New York: McGraw-

Hill, 1981, p. 504.
8. Quoted in Ted Ferguson, *Desperate Siege: The Battle of Hong Kong.* New York: Doubleday, 1980, p. 214.
9. Quoted in Noel Barber, "The Fall of Singapore," in *Reader's Digest Illustrated Story of World War II,* p. 42.
10. Quoted in the Editors of Time-Life Books, *WW II: Time-Life History of the Second World War.* New York: Barnes & Noble, 1995, p. 172.
11. Quoted in Stephen E. Ambrose and C. L. Sulzberger, *American Heritage New History of World War II.* New York: Viking, 1997, p. 143.
12. Quoted in Gordon W. Prange, with Donald M. Goldstein and Katherine V. Dillon, *Miracle at Midway.* New York: Penguin Books, 1982, p. 363.
13. Yuki Tanaka, *Hidden Horrors: Japanese War Crimes in World War II.* Boulder, CO: Westview Press, 1996, p. 195.
14. Quoted in Wheeler, *A Special Valor,* p. 130.
15. Quoted in Robert Leckie, "Tarawa: Conquest of the Unconquerable," in *Reader's Digest Illustrated Story of World War II,* p. 254.
16. Quoted in Clark G. Reynolds and the Editors of Time-Life Books, *The Carrier*

War. Alexandria, VA: Time-Life Books, 1984, p. 142.

17. Quoted in Clay Blair Jr., *MacArthur.* Garden City, NY: Doubleday, 1977, p. 175.

18. Quoted in Theodore Taylor, "Iwo Jima," in Desmond Flower and James Reeves, eds., *The War, 1939–1945: A Documentary History.* New York: Da Capo Press, 1997, p. 771.

19. Quoted in Nathan Miller, *War at Sea: A Naval History of World War II.* New York: Scribner, 1995, p. 526.

Chapter 2: Bataan and Corregidor: A Gallant Defense

20. Quoted in Warren J. Clear, "The Gallant Defense of the Philippines," in *Reader's Digest Illustrated Story of World War II,* p. 152.

21. Quoted in Blair, *MacArthur,* p. 38.

22. David G. Chandler, Colin McIntyre, and Michael C. Tagg, *Chronicles of World War II.* Godalming, UK: Bramley Books, 1997, p. 121.

23. Quoted in Chandler, McIntyre, and Tagg, *Chronicles of World War II,* p. 121.

24. Quoted in Ronald H. Spector, *Eagle Against the Sun: The American War with Japan.* New York: Free Press, 1985, p. 108.

25. Quoted in William Manchester, *American Caesar: Douglas MacArthur 1880–1964.* Boston: Little, Brown, 1978, p. 215.

26. Quoted in Manchester, *American Caesar,* p. 215.

27. Quoted in Manchester, *American Caesar,* p. 217.

28. Quoted in Manchester, *American Caesar,* p. 217.

29. Clear, "The Gallant Defense of the Philippines," p. 156.

30. Quoted in Chandler, McIntyre, and Tagg, *Chronicles of World War II,* p. 127.

31. Quoted in John Toland, *But Not in Shame: The Six Months After Pearl Harbor.* New York: Signet Books, 1962, p. 186.

32. Quoted in Blair, *MacArthur,* p. 67.

33. Quoted in Albert E. Cowdrey, *Fighting for Life: American Military Medicine in World War II.* New York: Free Press, 1994, p.40.

34. Quoted in Manchester, *American Caesar,* p. 237.

35. Quoted in Toland, *But Not in Shame,* p. 295.

36. Quoted in Toland, *But Not in Shame,* p. 327.

37. Clear, "The Gallant Defense of the Philippines," p. 157.

38. Quoted in John Costello, *The Pacific War 1941–1945.* New York: Quill, 1982, p. 262.

39. Quoted in Toland, *The Rising Sun,* vol. 1, p. 390.

40. Quoted in Blair, *MacArthur,* p. 81.

Chapter 3: Guadalcanal: The First U.S. Offensive

41. Quoted in Costello, *The Pacific War 1941–1945,* p. 314.

42. Quoted in Miller, *War at Sea,* p. 260.

43. Quoted in Miller, *War at Sea,* p. 263.

44. Quoted in Costello, *The Pacific War 1941–1945*, pp. 321–22.

45. Quoted in Chandler, McIntyre, and Tagg, *Chronicles of World War II*, p. 153.

46. Quoted in Spector, *Eagle Against the Sun*, p. 192.

47. Quoted in Spector, *Eagle Against the Sun*, p. 192.

48. Quoted in Moskin, *The Story of the U.S. Marine Corps*, p. 263.

49. Quoted in Wheeler, *A Special Valor*, p. 52.

50. Quoted in Wheeler, *A Special Valor*, p. 52.

51. Quoted in Costello, *The Pacific War 1941–1945*, p. 328.

52. Robert Leckie, *Helmet for My Pillow*. Garden City, NY: Doubleday, 1979, p. 71.

53. Quoted in Chandler, McIntyre, and Tagg, *Chronicles of World War II*, p. 154.

54. Quoted in Moskin, *The Story of the U.S. Marine Corps*, p. 266.

55. Quoted in Chandler, McIntyre, and Tagg, *Chronicles of World War II*, p. 158.

56. Hough, "Action at Guadalcanal, 'Island of Death,'" p. 219.

57. Quoted in Wheeler, *A Special Valor*, p. 101.

58. Quoted in Wheeler, *A Special Valor*, p. 103.

59. Quoted in Moskin, *The Story of the U.S. Marine Corps*, p. 273.

60. Quoted in Wheeler, *A Special Valor*, p. 105.

Chapter 4: Tarawa: Bloody Betio

61. Quoted in Leckie, "Tarawa: Conquest of the Unconquerable," p. 237.

62. Quoted in Costello, *The Pacific War 1941–1945*, p. 428.

63. Quoted in Miller, *War at Sea*, p. 397.

64. Quoted in Joseph H. Alexander, with Don Horan and Norman C. Stahl, *A Fellowship of Valor: The Battle History of the United States Marines*. New York: HarperCollins, 1997, p. 140.

65. Quoted in Spector, *Eagle Against the Sun*, p. 264.

66. Quoted in Costello, *The Pacific War 1941–1945*, p. 435.

67. Quoted in Spector, *Eagle Against the Sun*, p. 264.

68. Quoted in Alexander, *A Fellowship of Valor*, p. 147.

69. Quoted in Alexander, *A Fellowship of Valor*, p. 151.

70. Quoted in Moskin, *The Story of the U.S. Marine Corps*, p. 300.

71. Quoted in Moskin, *The Story of the U.S. Marine Corps*, p. 301.

72. Quoted in Miller, *War at Sea*, pp. 399–400.

73. Quoted in Costello, *The Pacific War 1941–1945*, p. 438.

74. Quoted in Wheeler, *A Special Valor*, p. 204.

Chapter 5: Leyte Gulf: The Greatest Naval Battle

75. Nathan Miller, *The Naval Air War 1939–1945*. Annapolis, MD: Naval Institute Press, 1991, p. 105.

76. Quoted in Cutler, *The Battle of Leyte Gulf 23–26 October 1944*, p. 56.

77. Quoted in Hanson W. Baldwin, "The Greatest Sea Fight: Leyte Gulf," in

Reader's Digest Illustrated Story of World War II, p. 458.

78. Quoted in Blair, *MacArthur*, p. 175.

79. Quoted in Miller, *War at Sea*, p. 461.

80. Quoted in Miller, *The Naval Air War 1939–1945*, pp. 170–71.

81. Quoted in Costello, *The Pacific War 1941–1945*, p. 509.

82. Quoted in Baldwin, "The Greatest Sea Fight: Leyte Gulf," p. 466.

83. Quoted in Baldwin, "The Greatest Sea Fight: Leyte Gulf," p. 466.

84. Quoted in Bernard Edwards, *Salvo! Classic Naval Gun Actions.* London: Arms & Armour Press, 1995, p. 183.

85. Quoted in Reynolds and the Editors of Time-Life Books, *The Carrier War*, p. 155.

86. Quoted in Toland, *The Rising Sun*, vol. 2, p. 712.

87. Quoted in Cutler, *The Battle of Leyte Gulf 23–26 October 1944*, pp. 59–60.

88. Quoted in Miller, *The Naval Air War 1939–1945*, p. 176.

89. Quoted in Costello, *The Pacific War 1941–1945*, p. 513.

90. Quoted in Costello, *The Pacific War 1941–1945*, p. 516.

91. Quoted in Cutler, *The Battle of Leyte Gulf 23–26 October 1944*, p. 264.

Chapter 6: Iwo Jima: Uncommon Valor

92. Quoted in Paul M. Kennedy, "Iwo Jima (1945)," in Jon E. Lewis, ed., *The Mammoth Book of Battles.* New York: Carroll & Graf, 1995, p. 390.

93. Quoted in Alexander, *A Fellowship of Valor*, p. 208.

94. Quoted in Moskin, *The Story of the U.S. Marine Corps*, p. 358.

95. Quoted in Costello, *The Pacific War 1941–1945*, p. 542.

96. Quoted in Costello, *The Pacific War 1941–1945*, p. 541.

97. Quoted in Alexander, *A Fellowship of Valor*, p. 212.

98. Quoted in Alexander, *A Fellowship of Valor*, p. 213.

99. Quoted in U.S. Marine Corps correspondent, "Iwo Jima, Pacific Ocean, 19 February 1945," in Jon E. Lewis, ed., *The Mammoth Book of Eye-Witness History*, New York: Carroll & Graf, 1998, pp. 459–60.

100. Quoted in Moskin, *The Story of the U.S. Marine Corps*, p. 364.

101. Quoted in Costello, *The Pacific War 1941–1945*, p. 546.

102. Quoted in Costello, *The Pacific War 1941–1945*, p. 546.

103. Quoted in Alexander, *A Fellowship of Valor*, p. 217.

104. Quoted in Toland, *The Rising Sun*, vol. 2, p. 826.

105. Quoted in Alexander, *A Fellowship of Valor*, p. 225.

Chapter 7: Okinawa: The Last Battle

106. Quoted in Edward Jablonski, *Airwar.* Vol. 2. Garden City, NY: Doubleday, 1971, p. 189.

107. Robert Leckie, *Okinawa: The Last Battle of World War II.* New York: Viking, 1995, p. 78.

108. Quoted in James H. Hallas, *Killing*

Ground on Okinawa: The Battle for Sugar Loaf Hill. Westport, CT: Praeger, 1996, p. 9.

109. Quoted in Miller, *War at Sea*, p. 516.
110. Quoted in Leckie, *Okinawa*, p. 64.
111. Quoted in Alexander, *A Fellowship of Valor*, p. 231.
112. Quoted in James Tobin, *Ernie Pyle's War: America's Eyewitness to World War II.* New York: Free Press, 1997, p. 2.
113. Quoted in Hallas, *Killing Ground on Okinawa*, p. 9.
114. Walter J. Boyne, *Clash of Wings: Air Power in World War II.* New York: Simon & Schuster, 1994, p. 273.
115. David Eggenberger, *An Encyclopedia of Battles: Accounts of Over 1,560 Battles from 1479 B.C. to the Present.* New York:

Dover, 1985, p. 317.
116. Quoted in Hallas, *Killing Ground on Okinawa*, p. 12.
117. Quoted in Hallas, *Killing Ground on Okinawa*, p. 13.
118. Quoted in Alexander, *A Fellowship of Valor*, p. 239.
119. Quoted in Wheeler, *A Special Valor*, pp. 413–14.
120. Quoted in Toland, *The Rising Sun*, vol. 2, p. 895.

Epilogue: The Atomic Age and Beyond
121. Quoted in Costello, *The Pacific War 1941–1945*, p. 591.
122. Quoted in Spector, *Eagle Against the Sun*, p. 555.

⋆ Glossary ⋆

banzai: Literally, "ten thousand years"; figuratively, when used in the context of a battle cry, "Hail to the Emperor! May he live for ten thousand years!"

banzai charge: A suicide charge.

BB: Battleship (USA).

B-29: Boeing four-engine long-range bomber; the "Superfortress."

Bushido or Bushido Code: Literally, "the Way of the Warrior"; the traditional warrior code of conduct, originally practiced by the samurai of medieval Japan and perpetuated in modified (some say corrupted) form by Japanese armed forces in the twentieth century.

CA: Heavy cruiser (USA).

CL: Light cruiser (USA).

CV: Fleet carrier (USA).

CVE: Escort carrier (USA).

CVL: Light carrier (USA).

DD: Destroyer (USA).

DE: Destroyer escort (USA).

Great Marianas Turkey Shoot: The Battle of the Philippine Sea.

gyokusai: Glorious self-annihilation; motivation for Japanese troops to fight to the death.

IJN: Imperial Japanese Navy.

kamikaze: "Divine wind"; name assigned to Japanese suicide pilots or planes during World War II.

kokutai: The national body through which Japanese warriors slain in combat purportedly lived on.

LCI: Landing craft, infantry (USA).

LCVP: Landing craft, vehicle, personnel (USA).

LSM: Landing ship, medium (USA).

LST: Landing ship, tank (USA).

LVT: Landing vehicle, tracked; also amtrac or amphtrac (USA).

rikusentai: Japanese Special Landing Force; elite troops, the Japanese equivalent of U.S. Marines.

samurai: Members of the warrior aristocracy of medieval Japan.

Sho: Japanese term for victory or "to conquer."

Sho Ichi Go: Operation Victory One; Japanese battle plan for the defense of the Philippines.

sortie: One flight by a single military plane.

strategy: The plan for an entire operation of a war or campaign.

tactics: The art of placing or maneuvering forces skillfully in a battle.

UDT: Underwater demolition team (USA).

USA: United States of America; United States Army.

USAAF: United States Army Air Force.

Yamato: Literally, "Great Peace"; the old name for Japan and a general term for the Japanese people; and one of Japan's super battleships.

★ Chronology of Events ★

1941

7 December: Japanese planes attack Pearl Harbor.

8 December: Japan declares war on the United States and Britain; bombs Philippines, Wake Atoll, and Guam; invades Thailand, Malaya (Malaysia), and Hong Kong.

9 December: Japanese troops land in Gilbert Islands.

16 December: Japan invades Borneo.

22 December: Japanese launch major offensive in Philippines.

23 December: Japanese capture Wake Atoll.

25 December: Fall of Hong Kong.

1942

2 January: Fall of Manila.

7 January–6:May: Battle of Bataan-Corregidor.

11 January: Japan invades Dutch East Indies.

8–15 February: Battle of Singapore.

27 February–1 March: Battle of the Java Sea.

9 March: Java surrenders.

13 March: Japanese troops land in Solomon Islands.

17 March: General Douglas MacArthur arrives in Australia from Philippines.

7–8 May: Battle of the Coral Sea.

4–7 June: Battle of Midway.

7 August– February 1943: Battle of Guadalcanal.

12–15 November: Naval Battle of Guadalcanal.

1943

21 February: U.S. troops secure Russell Islands.

2–4 March: Battle of the Bismarck Sea.

11–29 May: Battle of Attu (Aleutian Islands).

30 June: U.S. troops capture Rendova.

6 July: First Battle of Kula Gulf.

12–13 July: Second Battle of Kula Gulf.

27 October: U.S. troops seize Choiseul and the Treasury group.

1 November–25 March 1944: Battle of Bougainville.

20–23 November: Battle of Tarawa Atoll and Makin Island.

26–29 December: Battle of New Britain.

1944

1–4 February: Battle of Kwajalein Atoll.

17–24 February: Battle of Eniwetok Atoll.

18 February: U.S. naval air forces pummel Japanese installations on Truk Island in Caroline Islands.

22 April: U.S. troops land on Hollandia, Dutch New Guinea.

15 June: U.S. planes bomb Tokyo.

15 June–9 July: Battle of Saipan.

19–20 June: Battle of the Philippine Sea.

21 July–10 August: Battle of Guam.

24–31 July: Battle of Tinian.

15 September: U.S. troops land on Morotai in the northern Moluccas.

15 September–25 November: Battle of Peleliu-Angaur.

20 October–25 December: Battle of Leyte.

23–26 October: Battle of Leyte Gulf.

1945

9 January–1 July: Battle of Luzon.

19 February–26 March: Battle of Iwo Jima.

1 April–22 June: Battle of Okinawa.

6 August: U.S. drops atomic bomb on Hiroshima.

8 August: Soviet Union declares war on Japan.

9 August: U.S. drops atomic bomb on Nagasaki.

14 August: Japan accepts surrender terms.

15 August: Cease-fire in Asia and the Pacific.

2 September: Formal surrender ceremonies aboard battleship *Missouri* in Tokyo Bay.

☆ For Further Reading ☆

Joseph H. Alexander, *Utmost Savagery: The Three Days of Tarawa.* New York: Ivy Books, 1995. Complete, definitive account of the battle by a former marine officer and present military historian.

Clay Blair Jr., *Silent Victory: The U.S. Submarine War Against Japan.* 2 vols. Philadelphia: J. B. Lippincott, 1975. Comprehensive history of the submarine war against Japan.

Tom Brokaw, *The Greatest Generation.* New York: Random House, 1998. The story of American citizen heroes during World War II.

Harold L. Buell, *Dauntless Helldivers: A Dive-Bomber Pilot's Epic Story of the Carrier Battles.* New York: Bantam Doubleday Dell, 1991. Personal account of dive-bomber action during World War II.

Martin Caidin, *Zero Fighter.* Weapons Book No. 9, Ballantine's Illustrated History of World War II. New York: Ballantine Books, 1973. An exciting account of the agile World War II fighter plane.

Christopher Chant et al., *The Encyclopedia of Air Warfare.* New York: Thomas Y. Crowell, 1975. An illustrated history of war in the air.

Robert B. Edgerton, *Warriors of the Rising Sun.* New York: W. W. Norton, 1997. A chronicle of the Japanese military's transformation from honorable "knights of Bushido" into men who massacred thousands during the Pacific War.

John W. Lambert, *Bombs, Torpedoes, and Kamikazes.* North Branch, MN: Specialty Press, 1997. A pictorial history of kamikaze action during World War II.

Zenji Orita, with Joseph D. Harrington, *I-Boat Captain.* Canoga Park, CA: Major Books, 1978. A Japanese submarine captain writes about the undersea war in the Pacific.

Saburo Sakai, with Martin Caidin and Fred Saito, *Samurai!* New York: Ballantine Books, 1972. The story of Japan's war in the air, told by its greatest surviving fighter ace of World War II.

Russell Spurr, *A Glorious Way to Die: The Kamikaze Mission of the Battleship* Yamato, April 1945. New York: Newmarket Press, 1981. The death of Japan's greatest battleship.

★ Works Consulted ★

Joseph H. Alexander, with Don Horan and Norman C. Stahl, *A Fellowship of Valor: The Battle History of the United States Marines.* New York: HarperCollins, 1997. A single-volume, definitive history of the marines.

Stephen E. Ambrose and C. L. Sulzberger, *American Heritage New History of World War II.* New York: Viking, 1997. A masterful updating of the standard reference work.

Eric Bergerud, *Touched with Fire: The Land War in the South Pacific.* New York: Viking, 1996. Describes the horrors of this war through the eyes of its combatants.

Clay Blair Jr., *MacArthur.* Garden City, NY: Doubleday, 1977. A short, highly readable biography.

Walter J. Boyne, *Clash of Wings: Air Power in World War II.* New York: Simon & Schuster, 1994. Exciting air action in all wartime theaters.

David G. Chandler, Colin McIntyre, and Michael C. Tagg, *Chronicles of World War II.* Godalming, UK: Bramley Books, 1997. Selected accounts of great campaigns.

John Costello, *The Pacific War 1941–1945.* New York: Quill, 1982. Complete one-volume account of the causes and conduct of the Pacific War.

Albert E. Cowdrey, *Fighting for Life: American Military Medicine in World War II.* New York: Free Press, 1994. The revolution of medicine in World War II.

Thomas J. Cutler, *The Battle of Leyte Gulf 23–26 October 1944.* New York: Harper-Collins, 1994. The dramatic full story of the greatest naval battle in history.

Ernest Dupuy and Trevor Dupuy, *The Encyclopedia of Military History: From 3500 B.C. to the Present.* Rev. ed. New York: Harper & Row, 1986. The definitive one-volume work on military history; includes concise account of kamikaze operations.

Editors of Time-Life Books, *WW II: Time-Life History of the Second World War.* New York: Barnes & Noble, 1995. A condensation of Time-Life's thirty-nine-volume series.

Bernard Edwards, *Salvo! Classic Naval Gun Actions.* London: Arms & Armour Press, 1995. Detailed accounts of eighteen classic naval engagements.

David Eggenberger, *An Encyclopedia of Battles: Accounts of Over 1,560 Battles from 1479 B.C. to the Present.* New York: Dover, 1985. An excellent reference volume with ninety-nine battle maps.

Ted Ferguson, *Desperate Siege: The Battle of Hong Kong.* New York: Doubleday, 1980.

Describes how Hong Kong falls to the Japanese in the first month of the Pacific War.

Desmond Flower and James Reeves, eds., *The War, 1939–1945: A Documentary History*. New York: Da Capo Press, 1997. A mammoth digest of selected World War II writings.

James H. Hallas, *Killing Ground on Okinawa: The Battle for Sugar Loaf Hill*. Westport, CT: Praeger, 1996. The story of one of the lesser known but no less heroic battles fought by the U.S. Marines.

Edward Jablonski, *Airwar*. Vol. 2. Garden City, NY: Doubleday, 1971. An illustrated history of aerial warfare during World War II.

Raymond Lamont-Brown, *Kamikaze: Japan's Suicide Samurai*. London: Arms & Armour Press, 1997. Japan's determined last response to a war that was turning against it.

Robert Leckie, *Helmet for My Pillow*. Garden City, NY: Doubleday, 1979. The author's personal story of combat with the marines in the Pacific.

———, *Okinawa: The Last Battle of World War II*. New York: Viking, 1995. Leckie tells it as it was in smooth-flowing prose.

Jon E. Lewis, ed., *The Mammoth Book of Battles*. New York: Carroll & Graf, 1995. Gripping accounts of battles from the Boer War to the Gulf War.

———, ed., *The Mammoth Book of Eye-Witness History*, New York: Carroll & Graf, 1998. Firsthand accounts of history in the making from ancient times to the modern world.

The Library of America, *Reporting World War II. Part 2: American Journalism 1944–1946*. New York: Library Classics of the United States, 1995. An anthology of war reporting by some of America's finest reporters.

William Manchester, *American Caesar: Douglas MacArthur 1880–1964*. Boston: Little, Brown, 1978. Still the finest biography of the general available today.

Nathan Miller, *The Naval Air War 1939–1945*. Annapolis, MD: Naval Institute Press, 1991. Three distinct stages of the air-sea war are fully presented.

———, *War at Sea: A Naval History of World War II*. New York: Scribner, 1995. Captures the total naval war in the Pacific in one sweeping narrative.

J. Robert Moskin, *The Story of the U.S. Marine Corps*. New York: Paddington Press, 1979. A masterwork on the U.S. Marines by an award-winning journalist and historian.

Norman Polmar and Thomas B. Allen, *World War II: The Encyclopedia of the War Years 1941–1945*. New York: Random House, 1996. The definitive resource on the war from an American perspective.

Gordon W. Prange, with Donald M. Goldstein and Katherine V. Dillon, *At Dawn We Slept: The Untold Story of Pearl Harbor*. New York: McGraw-Hill, 1981. The definitive account of Japan's treachery at Pearl Harbor.

———, *Miracle at Midway*. New York: Penguin Books, 1982. Perhaps the best available history of the battle that turned the tide of the war in the Pacific.

Reader's Digest Illustrated Story of World War II. Pleasantville, NY: Reader's Digest Association, 1978. A comprehensive survey of World War II action and events.

Clark G. Reynolds and the Editors of Time-Life Books, *The Carrier War.* Alexandria, VA: Time-Life Books, 1984. Illustrated history of carrier-aircraft aerial action in World War II.

Ronald H. Spector, *Eagle Against the Sun: The American War with Japan.* New York: Free Press, 1985. A broad reassessment of U.S. and Japanese strategies during World War II offering some provocative interpretations.

Jack Stenbuck, ed., *Typewriter Battalion: Dramatic Frontline Dispatches from World War II.* New York: William Morrow , 1995. Actual words from war correspondents who reported day to day, battle by battle, from the war front in World War II.

Yuki Tanaka, *Hidden Horrors: Japanese War Crimes in World War II.* Boulder, CO: Westview Press, 1996. Documents hidden Japanese atrocities of World War II.

James Tobin, *Ernie Pyle's War: America's Eyewitness to World War II.* New York: Free Press, 1997. An affectionate yet critical biography of America's favorite war correspondent in World War II.

John Toland, *But Not in Shame: The Six Months After Pearl Harbor.* New York: Signet Books, 1962. An exciting account of the first six months of the Pacific War.

———, *The Rising Sun: The Decline and Fall of the Japanese Empire 1936–1945.* 2 vols. New York: Random House, 1970. A narrative history of Japan from the invasion of Manchuria to the atom bomb.

Richard Wheeler, *A Special Valor: The U.S. Marines and the Pacific War.* New York: Harper & Row, 1983. A vivid and complete account of marines at war in the Pacific.

Hiromichi Yahara, *The Battle for Okinawa.* New York: John Wiley & Sons, 1995. A Japanese officer's eyewitness account of the last great campaign of World War II.

★ Index ★

★ Picture Credits ★

Cover photo: Digital Stock
American Stock/Archive Photos, 51 (left)
Archive Photos, 36 (top), 42, 54, 61 (top), 76
Corbis, 22, 24, 27, 31, 35, 36 (bottom), 39, 40, 51 (right), 55, 61 (bottom), 64, 65, 66, 69 (right), 70, 79, 87 (top), 88
Corbis/Hulton-Deutsch Collection, 20, 57, 81, 86
Corbis-Bettmann, 15, 19, 25, 32, 33, 51 (center), 84
Digital Stock, 5, 7 (both), 10, 17 (both), 18, 34, 43, 47, 49, 58, 60, 69 (left), 73, 82, 87 (bottom), 92, 93
Library of Congress, 11
Lineworks, Incorporated, 21, 63
National Archives, 12, 74
Martha Schierholz, 38, 52, 77, 83
Steichen Combat Prints/United States Naval Academy, 91
U.S. Army Photo/FPG International, 72, 80

★ About the Author ★

Earle Rice Jr. attended San Jose City College and Foothill College on the San Francisco peninsula after serving nine years with the U.S. Marine Corps.

He has authored more than thirty books for young adults, including fast-action fiction and adaptations of *Dracula, All Quiet on the Western Front,* and *The Grapes of Wrath.* Mr. Rice has written seventeen books for Lucent, including *The Cuban Revolution, The Salem Witch Trials, The Final Solution, Nazi War Criminals, Life in the Middle Ages,* and two other books in the American War Library series, *Kamikazes* and *Strategic Battles in Europe.* He has also written articles, short stories, and miscellaneous website materials, and has previously worked for several years as a technical writer.

Mr. Rice is a former senior design engineer in the aerospace industry who now devotes full time to his writing. He lives in Julian, California, with his wife, daughter, two granddaughters, two cats, and a dog.